Applying More Inspiring Biographies from the Bible for Personal Growth:
Examining Patience, Wisdom, Peace, Enthusiasm and Commitment, Gratitude, and Happiness

Kimberly Mittendorf Hensley, MA, MEd

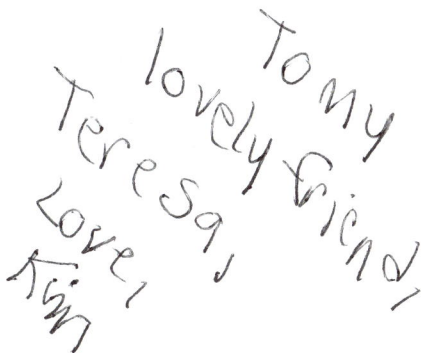

Copyright © 2016 Kimberly Mittendorf Hensley

All rights reserved.

ISBN-10: 1535037652
ISBN-13: 9781535037655

DEDICATION

This book is dedicated to my mother, Yvonne Mittendorf. Thanks, Mom, for all the Bible stories you read to me as a child. I appreciate the firm foundation.

CONTENTS

1	Their Stories Can Transform Your Story	1
2	Patience: I Will Wait Upon the Lord	9
3	Wisdom: Mining for Gold	21
4	Peace: Being a Mary in a Herod-Ruled World	33
5	Enthusiasm and Commitment: With All His Heart, With All Your Heart	39
6	Gratitude: Mary Magdalene Washes Feet and the Cleansed Leper Gives Thanks	47
7	Happiness: Found on a Road and Up a Tree	55
8	The Everlasting Story	65
	Endnotes	71
	About the Author	75

Unless otherwise indicated, all Scriptures are taken from *The Living Bible,* ©1971 owned by assignment by Illinois Regional Bank N.A. (as trustee). Used by permission of Tyndale House Publishers, Inc., Wheaton, Illinois 60189. All rights reserved.

Scripture references marked Message are taken from *The Message Bible* © 1993 by Eugene N. Peterson, NavPress, PO Box 35001, Colorado Springs, Co 80935, 4th printing in USA 1-994. Published in association with the literary agency – Alive Comm. PO Box 49068, Colorado Springs, CO 80949. Used by permission.

Scripture references marked NKJV are taken from the *New King James Version*, © 1979, 1980, 1982 by Thomas Nelson, Inc., Publishers Used by permission.

Scripture references marked AMP are taken from *The Amplified Bible, Old Testament,* © 1965 and 1987 by the Zondervan Corporation, and from *The Amplified New Testament,* ©1954, 1958, 1987 by the Lockman Foundation. Used by permission.

Scripture references marked KJV are taken from the *King James Version* of the Bible.

Also used T*he Life Recovery Bible* and *The Archeological Study Bible*

Dear reader,

You would help me greatly by reviewing this book on Amazon.com. Thank you for your support.

I would love to hear from you. My email address is khensley@zoomtown.com. My website is www.supportbykim.com. I am a certified life coach. Please let me know how I can help you.

Blessings,

Kimberly Mittendorf Hensley, Amelia, Ohio, November, 2016

1 THEIR STORIES CAN TRANSFORM YOUR STORY

"This Book of the Law shall not depart from your mouth, but you shall meditate in it day and night, that you may observe to do according to all that is written in it. For then you will make your way prosperous, and then you will have good success." (Joshua 1:8 NKJV)

The Bible can transform our lives. In this book, we will examine the patience of Job, the wisdom of Solomon, the peace of the mother of Jesus, Mary, the enthusiasm and commitment of Simon Peter, the gratitude of Mary Magdalene and a leper, and the happiness discovered by Paul and Zacchaeus. These stories can inform, encourage, and comfort us. In short, they can revolutionize our lives.

In chapter two, we will explore the saga of Job. This is a story of a good and honorable man who, even when suffering greatly without reason, chose to wait upon the Lord. The account of Job's experiences shows us how God can work in our lives to help us grow and mature. Trials can have a worthy purpose. They can help us develop patience.

We have a choice in how we react to trials. We must choose to believe the promises in the Word if we are to endure to the end. It is often very difficult to understand the misery that goes on in the world. Such misery becomes even more incomprehensible when it hits close to home.

But suffering will come in this fallen world and a decision must be made; will we react negatively or will we choose to trust in God's greater purpose even when we do not understand what is happening or why?

How we deal with suffering has enormous repercussions. It may determine whether we experience ultimate victory or defeat. If we can accept the suffering and choose to believe we will grow from it and become fashioned more into the likeness of Jesus through it, we can endure until victory arrives.

Let your faith thrive when you experience hard things that you do not understand. It will be very beneficial to you personally and will inspire those who are observing how you handle the tough parts of life.

Have the patience to continue pursuing your goals and dreams until you achieve them. No matter how difficult life becomes, never give up. Keep putting one foot in front of the other even amid bewildering pain and unanswered questions.

Job's story is one of a faithful believer being tested to the utmost. He came through it all triumphantly. You can too. No matter what it is you are wrestling with, patience will see you through.

Job's attitude throughout his trials was remarkable. He reasoned that God had given him everything he had. Therefore, He had the right to take it away at any time without explanation. Job's predominant sentiment throughout his ordeal remained, "Blessed be the name of the Lord."

Sometime, like Job's companions, our friends will lack insight about what we are going through. With them, also, we must be patient.

Shrouded in all of His mystery, God is so far beyond us that ultimately we are in no position to question His decisions. Like Job, we must simply and humbly bow before Him and shut our mouths.

Patience could be described as maintaining a sense of composure while suffering. It involves tolerating others when it is not easy to do so. It is a willingness to wait without irritation. It entails consistently reaching toward goals even when the going gets rough.

We can learn to apply patience to the particulars of our own individual lives. Jesus loves us completely and will never give up on us. That should give us the strength to be ever gentle with others as well as ourselves as we try our best to muddle through whatever life hands us.

Chapter three prospects the wisdom of Solomon. True sagacity is realizing is each moment that God is with us and is always available to help us. It is being as compassionate with others and ourselves as Jesus is.

God rewards our faith in Him. He does this not because we are worthy, but because we trust Him. It is not the seriousness of our problems that moves God on our behalf, it is our absolute belief in Him and His ultimate goodness. We must be sensible enough to fully place our problems in His loving hands. This is when we will experience His sweet deliverance.

Wisdom reveals strength at its best - a melding of knowledge and character; a union of cognition and virtue. Enlightenment, goodwill, sober judgment and the pursuit of excellence are some of the concepts that personify wisdom.

People with foresight look to the big picture. A prescient person is concerned with more than self-interest, focusing on the needs of others and the larger community. Wise people are caring and compassionate toward those around them because they understand that we are all connected. As Christians, in our unity we make up the body of Christ.

When Solomon succeeded his father, David, on the throne of Israel, he was greatly concerned for the welfare of the people he was to govern. When God gave Solomon the opportunity to make a request, the young ruler asked to be given wisdom to govern competently.

God was quite pleased with this request. He did give Solomon great understanding, and riches and honor besides.

Wisdom entails pondering the deeper meaning of life. It is realizing that there is a mysterious aspect to existence. Some questions have no easy answers.

Wisdom is having sound judgment, and the ability to give cogent advice. It is possessing exceptional comprehension and displaying equipoise when it matters most. It is acting with enlightenment and integrity. It is utilizing intelligence for the greater good.

There is much to be said for the value of common sense. Appropriate priorities and boundaries must be set if one is to be successful. Good relationships with others are critical. Such advice and more is expressed by Solomon in the book of Proverbs. Chapter three will look into the vast, unlimited knowledge of God and how it is worth its weight in gold.

Chapter four explores the majestic tranquility exhibited by our Lord's mother. An angel appeared to Mary and told her that the Holy Spirit would come upon her and that she would give birth to the blessed Son of God. Her immediate respond was to yield; she was prepared at once to serve in any way God desired.

We can learn much from Mary's quiet dignity. She always trusted God. She chose to depend upon Him completely. Her heart was not focused on her personal pain but rather on doing God's will.

Think of Mary at the foot of the cross. She watched her Son and Lord die an agonizing and cruel death. She endured the flowing blood, the anguish, and the excruciating pain her Son was experiencing. When we think of Jesus's crucifixion and Mary's silent suffering, we are encouraged to take up our own crosses, trusting in God's timing and larger purpose.

In 2 Timothy 2:22 we are told to, "pursue righteous living, faithfulness, love, and peace. Enjoy the companionship of those who call on the Lord with pure hearts."

Jesus, like His mother, exhibited these qualities. He possessed a remarkable quiescence as He solemnly lived and nobly died.

There was a larger purpose in Jesus's life and death, as there was in Mary's.

Mary chose to live in absolute trust, to bear her Son's and her own agony with remarkable self-possession.

If Mary was a pillar of tranquility, King Herod was a study in unrest. When the wise men were searching for the Christ child, they found their way to Herod's palace. Asking for directions, they ignited the king's insecurities. He did everything possible to destroy 'the King of the Jews' but succeeded only in destroying himself.

The singularly secure place that any of us can reside is in the arms of our Savior – letting Him shape and mold our lives as He sees fit in His perfect depth of understanding.

He is love and goodness personified. His thoughts are infinitely higher than ours. Still, we can try to fathom His ways by pondering that which is true and virtuous and praiseworthy.

Seeking the mind of Christ leads to security and rest. Studying the life of His mother, Mary, can teach us the importance of endurance, quiet strength, and gentleness.

Chapter five explores the larger than life characteristics of Simon Peter. Jesus loved this brash, passionate man dearly. He called Peter the very rock on which He would build His church.

Studying the life of Peter, we encounter a paragon of enthusiasm and commitment. He was far from perfect, but he was effective. We, too, can make a worthy contribution to Christ's kingdom though we are plagued with faults and weaknesses.

Think of it – Peter walked on water! What would be possible for us if we trusted Jesus that profoundly and kept our eyes as completely upon Him?

We must study His infallible Word and commune with Him continually in prayer. We must, like Him, be more concerned about others than our own self-interests…even to the extreme of shouldering a cross and being true to the end.

We each have a vital role to play in the body of Christ. We are part of the whole, yet we each have a unique purpose only we can fulfill.

We must know who we are in Christ and what we uniquely have to offer. Do you know your own temperament and special gifts? Are you using your capabilities fully? Do you pursue your purpose zestfully? Do you have infectious energy? Can you allow Peter's dynamism to inspire you to think big as you contemplate your life goals?

Peter's life story teaches us that there is no room for rigid perfectionism in the believer's life. We need to be able to get over our inevitable mistakes and get on with our calling.

Peter had this kind of resilience. After all, he denied his Lord three times. He had sworn complete allegiance to Jesus, but when things got treacherous, he caved in. Three times he declared that he did not even know Jesus.

This abdication came at a time when Jesus was at His most vulnerable. Jesus was going through the most excruciating experience of His entire life, and Peter failed to be there when he was needed the most.

Yet, Peter recovered from this devastating experience. He went on to usher in the Day of Pentecost. The Holy Spirit Himself descended upon all believers and Peter was at the helm. That's what can happen when we, like Peter, align ourselves with the Lord's purposes.

Peter was an uneducated nonprofessional. He was a mere crusty fisherman. Yet, because the Spirit dwelling within him, he was quite effective in spreading the Good News about the salvation available through believing in Jesus Christ.

Peter became a passionate and convincing preacher to Jews and Gentiles alike. He was on fire for the Lord. He blazed brightly, doing his Kingdom work with great earnestness. We would be wise to model our own behavior after such a sincere disciple - no matter what the cost.

Chapter six investigates the marvelous strength of gratitude. Two of the best examples of gratitude found in the Bible are that of Mary Magdalene and the cleansed Samaritan leper who came back to thank Jesus for healing him.

The importance of thanking God for His blessings cannot be overstated. We have so much to appreciate about our lives. If we take the time to think about the goodness all around us, we must give thanks.

But even beyond being grateful for the good things in life, we can be accepting when trials come. Trials can help us mature and empathize with others. As James wrote, we should count it all joy when encountering trials. If we can stay positive in the midst of difficulty, we can keep contributing.

Gratitude becomes a reality when we fully face the fact that we are sinners to the core, yet God still looks at us as having infinite value. No matter what mistakes we have made, no matter how far down into the pit we have fallen, God can lift us out of the muck and mire. He fully redeems us.

Mary Magdalene was in just such a quagmire when Jesus liberated her. This battered and bruised prostitute most likely felt worthless. Yet Jesus taught her that she was worth everything. He would have died on the cross if only to save her…or if only to save me…or if only to save you.

This scarred and reviled woman was so thankful to Jesus that she made an extravagant display of her love for her Savior. She broke open a priceless jar of expensive oil and anointed Jesus's feet with it. She then wiped His feet with her hair and her tears.

Her gesture was intimate. She held nothing back. She was sold out to Jesus. She knew what a sinner she was, but she also understood and embraced who she was in Christ. He restored her dignity once and for all. He does the same for all who will trust themselves to Him.

Oh, that we would be as notorious in our zeal for Christ as Mary Magdalene. We, too, are called to wash dirty feet. Any dirty feet will do. For when we wash the feet of the least of these, we wash His feet.

And then, just as at the Last Supper, we can allow the Holy Savior of all the world to wash our dirty feet. He can cleanse us from all unrighteousness and return us to a state as though we had never sinned. We may feel like an outcast before men, but in Him we are supremely loved and forever redeemed.

The Samaritan leper in Luke 17 was just such an outcast. He was one of ten lepers whom Jesus healed. He was the only non-Jew in the lot, and the only one who returned to thank and praise Jesus for curing him.

We, too, have a great deal for which to praise Jesus. Through His substitutionary work on the cross He paid our sin debt in full. He wiped out every transgression we have ever committed or ever will commit.

It should be easy to be grateful to God. It should be automatic, even reflexive. He is our magnificent God. He deserves all of our love and adoration.

Chapter seven takes a look at happiness found on a road and up a tree. It delves into the conversion of Saul to Paul on a Damascus road and celebrates the redemption of Zacchaeus after Jesus found him up in a sycamore tree.

Paul and Zacchaeus were transformed through encountering Christ. After being convicted of their wretchedness, they were set free by His presence.

Despite disastrous past decisions, they were each given a fresh start. Purpose, satisfaction, and happiness were suddenly within reach.

Both had the courage and humility to receive what Jesus had to offer. They trusted in Him and thus gleaned immediate and absolute forgiveness and salvation.

The same forgiveness and salvation are available to each of us. From Jesus' perspective, none of us are beyond redemption. Not one.

An arrogant Pharisee believing in the exclusivity of Judaism, Paul was fashioned by God to become a missionary to the Gentiles. He was irrevocably transformed from a vindictive abuser to a loving messenger of the redemption available in the person of Jesus Christ.

Indeed, all of us have sinned and fallen short of the glory of God. But because we put our trust in Christ, He freely and completely takes away our sins. This was why Paul could instruct followers in his letter to the Philippians to always be full of joy in the Lord.

Paul endured the trials of being beaten, jailed, and shipwrecked. Yet he was happy. He could rejoice through it all because he knew Jesus was with him.

He felt the Savior's sweet presence and so he could be happy anywhere under any circumstances. He knew that Christ was the source of his energy and delight.

Paul's hope was placed securely on a future of living eternally in union with Jesus. This lifted him up in a way that helped him surmount his trials and suffering.

As a follower of Christ, you can withstand the hardships of life just as Paul did. Knowing that your eternal destiny is secure, you can march into the future with confidence.

Zacchaeus learned that lesson and was released from greediness in order to demonstrate felicitous generosity. His journey from self-centeredness to caring for the needs of others was momentous.

After Jesus found him aloft in a sycamore tree and accompanied him home for a meal, Zacchaeus was overcome with glee. He had used his position as a tax collector to swindle others. But after his encounter with the Messiah, he gave half of all his goods to the poor and returned four times over everything he had ever stolen. How free and light his soul must have felt in that instant.

The Lord is waiting to be as gracious to you as he was in the lives of the characters examined in this book. Job ended up with much more than he had lost. Solomon was blessed with riches and fame in addition to the wisdom he had requested. Mary suffered greatly but had the high honor of being the mother of God's only begotten Son. Simon Peter was restored to faith and used mightily after denying Christ three times.

Mary Magdalene had the privilege of anointing Jesus's feet in preparation for His burial. She was also the first to see Him after His resurrection. The Samaritan leper was healed and had the satisfaction of expressing his deep gratitude to the Lord Himself. Paul became an evangelist to the very people he had formerly persecuted. Zacchaeus was empowered to leave his selfishness behind forever to become a generous giver and loyal follower of Jesus.

These colorful Bible characters teach us that we can be greatly used by God despite our misunderstandings, failures, and limitations. In encountering Jesus, each individual was completely transformed. Let their stories transform your story.

2 PATIENCE: I WILL WAIT UPON THE LORD

"My brethren, count it all joy when ye fall into divers temptations; knowing this, that the trying of your faith worketh patience. But let patience have her perfect work, that ye may be perfect and entire, wanting nothing." (James 1:2-4 KJV)

Would you agree that when the different aspects of your life are going well, you wish things would stay that way? Does anybody really want trials? When you are in the midst of acute suffering, do you secretly or openly beat your chest and ask, "Why, God, why?"

While we are on this earth, we may never fully know why people around the world have to endure abject misery. However, we see through a glass darkly. Clarity will come when we get to heaven.

After we receive the gift of salvation, which includes spending eternity with God, He works in our lives to grow us into mature and complete Christians. Trials help with that process. They help us acquire patience.

Notice that in the above Scripture, James did not write, "Let trials have their perfect work." Not at all! He wrote, "Let patience have her perfect work."[1]

In his book *31 Days of Healing*, Mark Brazee said, "You see, test and trials don't perfect you. It is what you do with them that matters. You are not perfected because a bunch of problems come along. You are perfected because you resolutely believe the Word of God in the midst of those problems and patiently endure. That's when patience has its perfect work."[2]

Patience may be defined as consistent endurance. No matter what happens to you, patience enables you to stay on an even keel.

The key to victorious, patient living comes by basing everything about your life on God's Word. Rather than looking to an internal thermometer and asking, "Who am I and how do I feel?" open the Word and let God tell you who you are and how to think.

Faithfulness through challenges accounts for the difference between success and failure. The way you choose to handle your problems determines whether you will live a triumphant life or give up in defeat. Rather than shrinking away from a challenge, allow faith to thrive in the midst of your suffering. This is the precise moment to put all your trust in

God. Standing firm, you can say, "I don't care what it looks like, seems like, sounds like, or feels like, I believe what the Word of God says!"3

Patience is both an aptitude (an ability you can acquire) as well as an attitude (a state of mind in regard to some matter). It is a strength. Displaying patience as a strength means you are firm in your will, character, and mind. You determine you will reach your goals and fulfill your purpose no matter what. By applying patience to each difficult life experience, you can inspire others and glorify God.

Of all the characters from the Bible, Job is certainly the most frequently linked to the virtue of patience. Job was a good man, careful to keep the Lord's commandments. Yet he suffered horribly. He never received a complete answer as to why he had to go through a living hell.

Those who read the book of Job understand that Satan perpetrated Job's fall into the pit of despair. Job 1 in *The Living Bible* translation opens: "There lived a man in the land of Uz, a man named Job – a good man who feared God and stayed away from evil." (v.1) The book says further that "he had a large family of seven sons and three daughters and was immensely wealthy." (v.2) He was scrupulous in prayer, never failing to thank God for his blessings and for giving his family protection. Overall, Job had a great life.

Enter the great besplatterer. According to verse 7 of the first chapter of Job, Satan, also called the Accuser, presented himself to God. God asked where Satan had come from. Satan replied that he had been watching everything on earth.

In verse 8, the Lord asked Satan, "Have you noticed my servant Job? He is the finest man in all the earth – a good man who fears God and will have nothing to do with evil."

"Why shouldn't he when you pay him so well?" Satan scoffed. "You have always protected him and his home and his property from all harm. You have prospered everything he does – look how rich he is! No wonder he 'worships' you! But just take away his wealth, and you'll see him curse you to your face!" (vv. 9-11)

The Lord decided He would prove Job's faithfulness by letting the devil test him. He allowed Satan to do anything except lay a finger on Job.

Almost immediately tragedy struck Job's household. A flurry of servants entered Job's home with bad news. The first servant informed Job that raiders had killed his donkeys and oxen, as well as all the farmhands. Another servant interrupted to say there had been a fire, and all the sheep and herdsmen had burned up.

Another servant entered and reported that three bands of Chaldeans had driven off Job's camels and killed the herdsmen. A final servant brought the devastating news that a mighty wind had swept in from the desert and collapsed the roof of the house where every one of Job's children had been eating. All of Job's children were dead.

"Then Job stood up and tore his robe in grief and fell down upon the ground before God, 'I came naked from my mother womb,' he said, 'and I shall have nothing when I die. The Lord gave me everything I had, and they were his to take away. Blessed be the name of the Lord.' In all of this, Job did not sin or revile God." (vv.20-22)

Soon after, God and Satan had another discussion in which God declared His pride in Job and how he handled the loss of his wealth and family. Satan retorted that Job would curse God if he lost his health. God told Satan to go right ahead and test Job again but to spare his life.

"So Satan went out from the presence of the Lord and struck Job with a terrible case of boils from head to foot. Then Job took a broken piece of pottery to scrape himself and sat among the ashes.

"His wife said to him, 'Are you still trying to be godly when God has done all this to you? Curse him and die.'

"But he replied, 'You talk like some heathen woman. What? Shall we receive only pleasant things from the hand of God and never anything unpleasant?' So in all this Job said nothing wrong." (2:7-10)

About this time, three of Job's friends - Eliphaz the Temanite, Bildad the Shuhite, and Zophar the Naamathite - arrived. They had heard of the tragedy that had befallen Job.

Job 2:12-13 explores their response to his trauma: "Job was so changed that they could scarcely recognize him. Wailing loudly in despair, they tore their robes and threw dust into the air and put earth on their heads to demonstrate their sorrow. Then they sat upon the ground with him silently for seven days and nights, no one speaking a word, for they saw that his suffering was too great for words."

Unfortunately, after the initial shock wore off, Job's friends began to pick at him. They suggested that he had committed some horrific sin that had brought this calamity upon him. From chapter 3 until halfway through the last chapter of Job, chapter 42, a philosophical discourse ensued between Job and his friends and between Job and God. In a series of long poetic soliloquies, all the major players weigh in with their opinions on the meaning of life and suffering.

Chapter 3 gives voice to Job's wish to die. In verses 2-10, Job lamented, "Let the day of my birth be cursed, and the night when I was conceived. Let that day be forever forgotten. Let it be lost even to God, shrouded in eternal darkness. Yes, let the darkness claim it for its own, and may a black cloud overshadow it. May it be blotted off the calendar, never again to be counted among the days of the month of that year. Let the night be bleak and joyless. Let those who are expert at cursing curse it. Let the stars of the night disappear. Let it long for light but never see it, never see the morning light. Curse it for its failure to shut my mother's womb, for letting me be born to come to all this trouble."

Rather than giving Job the comfort he so desperately needed at this dark juncture, Eliphaz lectured Job. In chapter 4 he accused Job of being faint and broken, whereas in the past Job had counseled many an afflicted soul to trust in God when trouble struck. Eliphaz's "sermon" continued through all of chapter 5. He repeatedly asserted that God was punishing Job for some sin. His advice to Job to repent echoes throughout all the coming chapters.

None of Job's friends believed he was innocent. Can you imagine how frustrating this must have been for Job? Yet he held his own. He had, as they say, "the patience of Job."

Job's reply to Eliphaz lasts through chapters 6 and 7 – "One should be kind to a fainting friend, but you have accused me without the slightest fear of God." (6:14)

In chapter 8, Bildad had his say. "If you were pure and good, God would hear your prayer and answer you and bless you with a happy home." (v.6)

Beyond chastising Job, Bildad waxed philosophical, as did all the main characters in the rest of the story: "Read the history books and see – for we were born but yesterday and know so little: our days here on earth are as transient as shadows. But the wisdom of the past will teach you. The experience of others will speak to you, reminding you that those who forget God have no hope. They are like rushes without any mire to grow in; nor grass without water to keep it alive." (vv.8-12)

Bildad insinuated that Job had forgotten God and therefore God was punishing him. Job's response in chapters 9 and 10 allowed him to express his frustration not only with Bildad but also with God. In Job 10:8, Job pled with the Lord, "You have made me, and yet you destroy me. Oh, please remember that I'm made of dust."

Next Zophar took his turn in chiding Job: "Before you turn to God and stretch out your hands to me, get rid of your sin and leave all iniquity behind you. Only then, without the spots of sin to defile you, can you walk steadily forward to God without fear. Only then can you forget your misery. It will all be in the past. And your life will be cloudless, any darkness will be as bright as morning." (11:13-17)

Imagine how Job felt when his friends spoke that way. Their words must have left such a bad taste in his mouth! Job's reply stretched from chapter 12 through chapter 14. He defended himself by saying, "This is my case: I know I am righteous…O God, there are two things I beg you not to do to me; only then will I be able to face you. Don't abandon me. And don't terrify me with your awesome presence." (13:18, 20-21)

The argument continues chapter by chapter. In chapter 30, we find Job still suffering terribly in addition to dealing with the barbs of his accusers. He cried, "My skin is black and peeling. My bones burn with fever. The joy and gladness has turned to mourning." (30:30-31)

In chapter 32, the last character in the drama, Elihu entered and enjoyed listening to himself talk so much that he carried on through chapter 37. Basically, he set himself up as someone with an upright heart who spoke sincerely, and yet he accused Job of being prideful for making the same claim. Like Job's other friends, Elihu assumed that external circumstances served as a measuring stick for the quality of a person's faith. He concluded that if Job was suffering, he was getting what he deserved.

Yet Elihu's assumptions were ridiculously off target. Job's trials were not a consequence of sinful living. In reality, they were a testimony of God's belief and trust in his beloved servant.

In Elihu's opinion, God was a kind of dictator who watches our actions, takes note of our deeds, and punishes us without need of further examination. This is not an accurate portrayal of our God. God did not accuse Job as his friends did. Satan was Job's accuser.

God is infinitely patient, slow to anger and quick to forgive. He looks at the heart. Anyone who sincerely submits to God through his son, Jesus Christ, will find Him merciful.

In chapters 38 through 41, the Lord appeared in a whirlwind and answered Job's entreaties. In eloquent and lyrical prose, God used a series of questions to show how little Job knew about creation and God's ways:

"Where were you when I laid the foundations of the earth? Tell me, if you know so much. Do you know how its dimensions were determined, and who did the surveying? What supports its foundations, and who laid its cornerstone as the morning stars sang together and all the angels shouted for joy?

"Who decreed the boundaries of the seas when they gushed from the depths? Who clothed them with clouds and thick darkness and barred them by limiting their shores, and said, 'Thus far and no farther shall you come, and here shall your proud waves stop!'?

"Have you ever once commanded the morning to appear and caused the dawn to rise in the east? Have you ever told the daylight to spread to the ends of the earth, to end the night's wickedness? Have you ever robed the dawn in red, and disturbed the haunts of wicked men, and stopped the arm raised to strike?

"Have you explored the springs from which the seas come, or walked in the sources of their depths? Has the location of the gates of Death been revealed to you? Do you realize the extent of the earth? Tell me about it if you know! Where does the light come from and how do you get there? Or tell me about the darkness. Where does it come from? Can you find its boundaries, or go to its source? But of course you know all this! For you were born before it was all created, and you are so very experienced!

"Have you visited the treasuries of the snow, or seen where hail is made and stored? For I have reserved it for the time when I will need it in war. Where is the path to the distribution point of light? Where is the home of the east wind? Who dug the valleys for the torrents of rain? Who laid out the path for the lightning, causing the rain to fall upon the haven deserts, so that the parched and barren ground is satisfied with water and tender grass springs up?" (vv. 4-27)

Job knew nothing of God's mysteries, so he could not comprehend God's character accurately. We also wonder why we suffer. We wonder why bad things happen to us, to our families, to all of humanity. We must realize God's ways are infinite while we are simple and finite creatures. The wisest thing we can do in our challenges and trials is to praise God and wait on His deliverance.

In chapter 40, the Lord asked Job, "Do you still want to argue with the Almighty? Or will you yield? Do you – God's critic – have the answers?" (v.2)

Then Job replied to God, "I am nothing – how could I ever find the answers? I lay my hand upon my mouth in silence. I have said too much already." (vv. 4-5)

Job's answer to God overflowed with gratitude, explained *The Life Recovery Bible*: "Where Job had once only heard about God, here he actually saw him

– the loving, merciful, all-powerful, majestic Creator. This man, who was known as 'blameless and upright' before his suffering, was now even greater because of that suffering. God is good. He gives us good gifts; He works good from all things; and His intentions for us are always good. Pain is a privilege when it leads us closer to God."4

After Job and God came to an agreement, God gave Job's so-called friends a good tongue-lashing. He was angry with them, telling them they had greatly blundered in what they had said about Him. He instructed them to present a burnt offering of bulls and rams as an act of contrition. He said Job would pray for them. He further decreed He would accept Job's prayer on their behalf rather than destroy them for their failure to speak appropriately to Job.

These pseudo-philosophers learned a lesson – friends in trouble need comfort and understanding, not judgment. Sometimes people choose to analyze rather than empathize because it is so very scary to put ourselves in the sufferer's position. In the back of our minds, at least on the subconscious level, we realize the same fate could befall us.

It is heartwarming to note that Job did not say one judgmental thing about how terribly unfairly his friends had treated him. No, he was quick to forgive and grant them mercy.

At this critical juncture, Job was the epitome of patience. Billy Graham described it in his book, *The Holy Spirit: Activating God's Power in Your Life*: "Patience is the transcendent radiance of a loving and tender heart which, in its dealings with those around it, looks kindly and graciously upon them. Patience graciously, compassionately and with understanding judges the faults of others without unjust criticism…Patience is a part of true Christlikeness."5

Surely this patience that enveloped Job's whole being was one of the reasons God felt so tenderly toward him. When Job prayed for his friends, the Lord restored Job's wealth and happiness. In actuality, He gave Job a double recompense for all he had lost.

Then all of Job's kin and friends gathered to give him a big party because God had brought him through his trials. Then God blessed him with enormous numbers of sheep, camels, teams of oxen, and female donkeys. He also gave Job seven more sons and three more daughters.

Chapter 42 concludes with this happy ending: "And in the end there were no other girls as lovely as the daughters of Job; and their father put them in his will along with their brothers. [Hurray for girl power and women's rights!] Job lived another 140 years, long enough to see his grandchildren and even his great-grandchildren. At last he died, an old, old man, after living a long, good life." (vv. 15-17)

I love the dramatic manner in which Job is written. It reads with such lovely lyricism and poignancy. The soliloquies hold the reader's interest creatively and effectively.

The most interesting aspect of the book to me is that Job displays all kinds of negative emotions to God and yet he is greatly known for his patience. Isn't it fascinating that God did not expect Job to suffer in silence and play the martyr? No, God respected Job's frank response to what he perceived to be a very unfair situation.

We live out our years in a world where injustice and unfairness seem to predominate. Through no fault of his own, Job lost his possessions, family, and health. He never got a clear answer as to why. In his struggles, though, he came to know God in a more mature and profound way. As you and I face unfairness in our lives, we can still make it an opportunity to learn more about how to trust in our perfect, loving, and all-knowing God.

God is so far above our deepest thoughts. Often we are unable to fathom His mysterious ways. Surely Job wondered why he had to suffer so much. It would have been easy for Job to reject God for the seeming injustice of it all. Yet Job believed that God was good. Despite lapses of despair and anger, Job trusted that in the end God would deal with him justly. He trusted God unconditionally.

The Life Recovery Bible says, "When life is going smoothly, trust is easy. The test of trust always comes when life stops making sense. Job gave us a very real example of how trust needs to work in our lives. Everything that Job enjoyed had been stripped away for no reason that he could understand. In spite of this, however, Job never gave up on God. He never placed hope in his experience, his wisdom, his friends, or his wealth. His trust was in God, even though he couldn't understand everything he went through. God alone is sufficient to help us with the ambiguities in life. We can trust in Him."[6]

God is in control of the universe. If we surrender to His plan for us, He will take charge of our lives and reward us both here on earth and in eternity. The future blessings that await us are greater than anything we can imagine.

Yes, being patient now will give us wonderful blessings throughout eternity. Yet God does not expect us to show a stiff upper lip and passively accept pain without complaining and seeking solace. In our character study of Job, we discover that it is all right to cry, doubt, fear, question, need, and wrestle with the very essence of our existence.

As our hearts cry against injustice and affliction, Job's saga reassures us that God wants us to be honest with Him. He wants us to communicate our true feelings to Him, even if that means expressing our anger. Being our Abba (Father), he wants us to run to Him when we are afraid. He can handle the strongest of emotions. They don't threaten or disappoint Him.

God longs for us to share our true selves with Him. He wants to participate with us even in the darkest times – especially then! He wants us to relate to Him as a whole person. This sets things into motion for Him to release the healing and hope He yearns to give us. Our God is the supreme example of true patience. Certainly Job's story helps us realize that the patience God calls us to exhibit is more complex than we might have superficially understood.

Wikipedia.org defines *patience* as, "The state of endurance under difficult circumstances. This can mean persevering in the face of delay or provocation without becoming annoyed or upset; or exhibiting forbearance when under strain, especially when faced with longer-term difficulties. It is also used to refer to the character trait of being steadfast."[7]

Patience is often described as a core virtue in religious practices. Job's story is noted in research as a profound religious work. According to Wikipedia: "At its core, the theme is the co-existence of evil and God and the application of patience is highlighted as the antidote to the earthly struggles caused by that co-existence. The plot of the book is that Job endures near-apocalyptic calamities without losing his patience or reproaching Divine Providence."[8]

Wikipedia continues, "In the Christian religion, patience is one of the most valuable virtues of life. Increasing patience is viewed as the work of the Holy Spirit in the Christian who has accepted the gift of salvation…patience is considered one of the seven virtues."[9]

The philosopher Friedrich Nietzsche said, "Being able to wait is so hard that the greatest poets did not disdain to make the inability to wait the theme of their poetry." Nietzsche cited Shakespeare's Othello and Sophocles' Ajax as literary examples of men so enflamed by their emotions that they refused to cool down and delay the instant gratification of acting out on their passions.[10]

Those of us who live in the United States can understand Jim Rohn's indictment that, "Americans are incredibly impatient. Someone once said that the shortest period of time in America is the time between when the light turns green and when you hear the first horn honk." He concluded that the twin killers of success are impatience and greed.11

A person is best able to be patient and giving when he or she is experiencing what Csikszentmihalyi and Nakamura call *flow*. This state is experienced when perceived challenges and skills are both just above average levels. You have most likely experienced flow when working on a demanding but exciting project in an area in which you have talent. When challenges or skills are way below or way above average levels, apathy is experienced. If the project is either so simple to you as to be boring or so difficult as to seem insurmountable, it is highly unlikely flow will occur. 12

Experiencing flow encourages a person to persist at and return to an activity because it is experientially rewarding. Each rewarding experience fosters the growth of skill over time. Children and adults who are able to habitually spend time in the flow zone would predictably have greater self-esteem than those who cannot. Mastering challenges in daily life protects against negative outcomes.13

Evidence suggests a relationship exists between quality of experience and persistence in an activity. Professional athletes provide a good example of flow. In a game, the challenges are high but so is the athlete's skill. Those of us who are not super-gifted athletically would find the game highly challenging, but we would not have the high skill to master it as the pro does.14

But each of us can achieve flow in the areas we are strong in. Think about your strengths. Can you remember times when you got so involved with what you were doing that time seemed to stop and fly by all at the same time? If you enjoy an experience and it is of quality for you, you would predictably have the patience to stick with it. You would enjoy working on the project for a longer time than someone for whom the activity does not suit his or her strengths very well.

I have to pause here a minute and insert another hurrah for girl power. Do you realize that women have larger prefrontal cortexes than men? It is true. This part of a woman's brain matures earlier than a man's. This is why women tend to have more patience than men.15

Psychologist Robert Emmons reported that patience "enables people to be attentively responsive to others, to be responsive to opportunities for goal attainment."16

Four primary meanings of patience are proposed: suffering with calmness and composure, forbearance and tolerance of others, willingness to wait without resentment, and constancy and consistency in effort. Patience is actually a necessary condition for the accomplishment of anything worthwhile.17

So what conditions tend to produce patience? "Engagement of effort requires both a goal that matters enough (value) and also sufficient confidence in its eventual attainment (expectancy)," say Carver and Scheier.18

We exhibit patience by refusing to give up. We have to be persistent to overcome obstacles. To demonstrate that consistency we must have confidence that we will eventually succeed in our endeavors.

Can you think of some examples of patience? Carver and Scheier offer, "The struggling student may work for months toward the completion of a project that is very difficult. People return to rebuild their homes in war-torn territories. The ability of people to struggle forward, to persevere against great odds even in the face of failure, represents a very important human strength."19

Paul commended the Thessalonians for their patience: "We are happy to tell other churches about your patience and complete faith in God, in spite of all the crushing troubles and hardships you are going through." (2 Thessalonians 1:4)

Christian writer Rick Renner elaborated in *Sparkling Gems from the Greek*, "The word *patience* is a favorite word in Paul's epistles. It is the compound Greek word, *hupomene*, and it paints the picture of one who is under a heavy load but refuses to bend, break, or surrender because he is convinced that the territory, promise, or principle under assault rightfully belongs to him. The word denotes a refusal to give up and an attitude that is determined to receive what is promised or hoped for. The King James Version translates it *patience*, but a better rendering would be *endurance*."20

It is important to realize we have to be just as patient with ourselves and our own foibles as we are with others. St. Francis de Sales suggested, "Have patience with all things, but chiefly have patience with yourself...Every day begin the task anew."

Life is messy and unpredictable. We might as well embrace it. People bumble through life the best they can. We must be merciful toward others. And we desperately need to extend that mercy to ourselves. We must look upon ourselves with the compassion Jesus extends.

What might happen if we treated ourselves in the tender, gentle manner a loving mother displays toward her newborn? The more love and mercy we shower on ourselves, the more patience flows from our innermost being to our family, friends, and people in need.

We have looked at the attribute of patience to discern ways we can incorporate it into our everyday lives. In this hyper world, it is advantageous to slow down. We must be willing to wait for what we want. We must be willing to persevere until we successfully complete what we were meant to accomplish in life.

You have distinct strengths. You have a unique destiny to fulfill. God made us all with different gifts so that we might effectively work together as a unified body. Moderate your pace so that you can enjoy your interactions with your brother and sisters in Christ. Take a little extra time to play with a child and tell him or her about Jesus. Smile and say hello to the people you meet on the street. Visit the sick and infirm. Make sure you display the fortitude of Jesus to the non-Christians who are watching you.

Water and tend to the good seeds in your life. Have the patience to wait for the seeds to germinate and grow into a fruitful orchard. As you embark on the adventure that is the rest of your life, take patience as your personal virtue that you might thrive and flourish.

3 WISDOM: MINING FOR GOLD

"Have you ever come on anything quite like this extravagant generosity of God, this deep, deep wisdom? It's way over our heads. We'll never figure it out. Is there anyone around who can explain God? Anyone smart enough to tell him what to do? Anyone who has done him such a huge favor that God has to ask his advice? Everything comes from him; everything happens through him; everything ends up with him. Always glory! Always praise! Yes. Yes. Yes." (Romans 11: 33-36 Message)

Sometimes we can lose our way and forget the awesomeness of the wonderful God who wishes to travel with us throughout life's journey. As we explore the life of Solomon we see many facets of our own humanity.

Although Solomon at times lost his way by worshipping the gods of his foreign wives, he was smart enough to ask God for the gift of wisdom. He also built a spectacular temple to honor the Lord.

Jehovah is worth every honor we can give Him. He is wisdom incarnate. He is the alpha and the omega; He is glorious and praiseworthy; He is perfect. He knows all things – and He wants to share that wisdom with us. All we have to do is invite Him into our lives.

Gaining divine wisdom is a freeing experience. In Hosea 6, God declared, "I desire mercy and not sacrifice, and the knowledge of God more than burnt offerings." (v.6)

God prefers to relate to us as a loving father more than as an angry judge. Often we hear an angry judge inside our heads and think it is God. It is not. It is our own ego tearing us to shreds.

"If we could see how harshly we judge ourselves and how much we expect of ourselves, we would see that's not helping us accomplish what we want to," says Jenifer Westphal, quoted in *What Happy Women Know*. "It's actually letting go of judgment, coming to yourself, and saying, 'I'm an awesome person who is contributing much to my family, to my spouse, and to my friends' that takes you to a happy place where you can start to get things done."[1]

Whatever challenges you are facing, you can get going in the right direction by looking at yourself as primarily worthy rather than as unworthy. God doesn't want you to think poorly of yourself. He wants you to reach out to Him in belief – to call those things that are not as though they were. He wants you to write a different story for your life, a story in which you do much good and have a great life. When you allow Him to be the author and finisher of that story, unimaginable dreams become a reality. God blesses you based upon your faith in Him, not on your neediness.

You can be as needy and messed up as is humanly possible, but if you do not have the wisdom to turn it all over to God, you will not receive the blessing. When you believe in God, you can begin to realize who you are through His eyes. This is how you become capable of living out the special calling that He has for your life.

To discover that calling, be a seeker willing to swim into as yet unknown spiritual depths to find it. "The search for human strengths is a continuous journey with a long history," says Ute Kunzmann in *Positive Psychology in Practice*. "Since antiquity, one of the guideposts in this search has been the concept of wisdom. At the core of this concept is the...integration of knowledge and character, mind and virtue...wisdom identifies in the most universal sense the highest forms of expertise that humans can acquire. Studying wisdom helps reveal the strongest qualities of humans as they have evolved through the experience of succeeding generations."[2]

Wisdom is such a powerful strength. It is a fusion of enlightenment, goodwill, sober judgment, and the pursuit of excellence. It takes into account the broader view of the big picture. It values not only the interests of the self but takes into account the interests of others as well.

"Wisdom is knowledge," Kunzmann continues, "about ways of developing ourselves not only without violating others' rights but also with co-producing resources for others to develop...a central characteristic of a wise person is the ability to translate knowledge into action geared toward the development of self and others...wise persons tend to be benevolent, compassionate, caring, and interested in helping others."[3]

How can we not thirst for this wonderful gift called wisdom? Don't we all want to possess a solid understanding of life, a sterling character, a sound mind, and a virtuous spirit? How could we possibly desire to go through life without learning to be a compassionate and caring person? Fortunately, we have an example to turn to in this quest.

One man in the Bible fully exemplified wisdom. His name was Solomon. Wikipedia explained that according to Jewish tradition, King Solomon wrote three books of the Bible: Mishlei – the book of Proverbs, a collection of fables and shirim, judicious sayings; Kohelet – Ecclesiastes, a book of contemplation and self-reflection; and Shir ha- Song of Songs, a collection of poetry and verse.[4]

Solomon was the second child conceived by King David and Bathsheba. Their first child had been a result of an adulterous relationship while Bathsheba's husband, Uriah, had been in battle. That baby died as a punishment for David's decision to put Uriah on the front lines to be killed in an attempt to hide the adultery and the pregnancy that resulted.

Out of that terrible beginning, the couple chose to try again. 2 Samuel 12:24-25 explained, "Then David comforted Bathsheba, his wife, and slept with her. She became pregnant and gave birth to a son, and David named him Solomon. The Lord loved the child and sent word through Nathan the prophet that they should name him Jedidiah (which means 'beloved of the Lord')."

When King David died there was a fierce battle about who would take the throne. It had been promised to Bathsheba's son, and she, with the help of the prophet Nathan, succeeded in placing Solomon on the throne.

As he ascended to kingship, David charged Solomon to obey God's laws and to "follow all his ways." (1 Kings 2:3) Solomon listened and obeyed his father. When given a choice of gifts from God, he humbly asked for wisdom.

1 Kings 3 tells the story of how God gave Solomon the opportunity to ask and receive anything he wished:

"Solomon replied, 'You were wonderfully kind to my father David because he was honest and true and faithful to you, and obeyed your commands. And you have continued your kindness to him by giving him a son to succeed him. Oh, Lord, my God, now you have made me the king instead of my father, David, but I am as a little child who doesn't know his way around. And here I am among your own chosen people, a nation so great that there are almost too many people to count! Give me an understanding mind so that I can govern your people well and know the difference between what is right and what is wrong. For who by himself is able to carry such a heavy responsibility?'

"The Lord was pleased with his reply and was glad that Solomon had asked for wisdom. So he replied, 'Because you have asked for wisdom in governing my people and haven't asked for a long life, or riches for yourself, or the defeat of your enemies – yes, I'll give you what you asked for! I will give you a wiser mind than anyone else ever had or ever will have! And I will give you what you didn't ask for – riches and honor! And no one in all the world will be as rich and famous as you for the rest of your life! And I will give you a long life if you follow me and obey my laws as your father David." (1 Kings 3:6-14)

Solomon received this wisdom because he carefully considered how God could best bless him and those he led. In *The Richest Man Who Ever Lived: King Solomon's Secrets to Success, Wealth, and Happiness*, Steven Scott pointed out, "Just as there are physical laws that govern the physical universe, Solomon reveals 'laws of living' that invisibly govern all aspects of life."5 These "laws of living" collectively make up the concept of wisdom.

Solomon was a diplomat, a trader, a collector, and a patron of the arts. He was also a botanist, a zoologist, an architect, a poet, and a philosopher.

He displayed his creativity in building the temple his father had so fervently dreamed of erecting. When David's loyal friend, King Hiram of Tyre, congratulated Solomon on ascending to the throne, Solomon sent the following message back to him:

"You know that my father, David, was not able to build a Temple to honor the name of the LORD his God because of the many wars waged against him by surrounding nations. He could not build until the LORD gave him victory over all his enemies. But now the LORD my God has given me peace on every side; I have no enemies, and all is well. So I am planning to build a Temple to honor the name of the LORD my God, just as he had instructed my father, David. For the LORD told him, 'Your son, whom I will place on your throne, will build the Temple to honor my name.'" (1 Kings 5: 3-5)

1 Kings 6 opened with this explanation; "It was in mid-spring…during the fourth year of Solomon's reign, that he began to construct the Temple of the LORD. This was 480 years after the people of Israel were rescued from their slavery in the land of Egypt." (v. 1)

Chapter six concluded that, "The building was completed in every detail by mid-autumn …during the eleventh year of his reign. So it took seven years to build the Temple." (v. 38)

In addition to his care with details concerning the building of the Temple, Solomon was also knowledgeable about mining. His mines represented a great portion of his wealth. He often used mining references in his writings. Proverbs 8:19 is a good example: "My fruit is better than gold, even fine gold, and my yield than choice silver." (ESV)

In his asking God for wisdom, we see Solomon's love of learning. In his writings, we find an open-mindedness in which he was willing to look at situations from many angles.

As a judge, Solomon demonstrated his supreme mastery of perspective when two women came to him with an issue. Both claimed to be the mother of the infant they brought before him. Solomon thought for a moment and offered to cut the baby in half. Of course, the real mother would not hear of this outrageous behavior, thus proving she was the rightful parent.

We expect to find the following four factors in wise people such as Solomon: First, the wise person comprehends the nature of human existence and tries to learn from his mistakes.

Second, the wise person knows when to give and when to withhold advice. He is a person others would go to for help with problems. Sometimes it is not yet the season for God's plan to come to fruition so the wise person must be aware of God's timing as he counsels people.

Third, the wise person knows that life's priorities may change and there can be possible conflicts among different life domains. A child would need to be supported in an entirely different way than a senior adult. Their maturity levels and interests would be quite dissimilar.

Also, at some junctures in life there will be clashes of duties for a person. Consider the working mom who is also trying to go back to college. The wise person must take all of this into account as he or she guides and mentors.

Fourth, the wise person has an exceptional personality and social functioning. He or she is a good listener and a very humane person.[6]

Some significant factors that exemplify wisdom include: addressing important and difficult questions and strategies about the conduct and meaning of life; recognizing the limits of knowledge and the uncertainties of the world; representing a truly superior level of knowledge, judgment, and advice; demonstrating knowledge with extraordinary scope, depth, measure, and balance; displaying a perfect synergy of mind and character, that is, an orchestration of knowledge and virtues; and finally, using knowledge for the good or well-being of oneself and that of others.

Though difficult to achieve and to specify, wisdom is easily recognized when manifested.[7] Isn't it pretty evident to us all when someone is judicious and perceptive?

As we look at the wisdom Solomon shared in Proverbs, note that what he wrote always met the criteria expressed above. There are several themes in the thirty-one chapters that make up the book of Proverbs.

It is obvious from his writing that Solomon held common sense in very high esteem. He emphasized the power of setting priorities that reflect

God's will in our lives. He explored how vital it is to set boundaries and to have the ability to say no. He also firmly endorsed building and maintaining healthy relationships.

In Proverbs 1:2-3, we discover that King Solomon wrote Proverbs so that the people of Israel would know how to live justly, fairly, and with understanding in every circumstance. He specifically mapped out how to live a good life, emphasizing that wisdom begins by revering and trusting in God.

This brings with it the implicit understanding that we need God's guidance and care. We learn that living with wisdom gives us a level of protection the foolish person will never possess.

Proverbs 1:20 affirmed, "Wisdom shouts in the streets for a hearing." It demands our attention. Those who heed it will be successful because wisdom comes from God.

In Proverbs 3:21-26 we read: "Have two goals: wisdom – that is, knowing and doing right – and common sense. Don't let them slip away, for they fill you with living energy and bring you honor and respect. They keep you safe from defeat and disaster and from stumbling off the trail. With them on guard you can sleep without fear; you need not be afraid of disaster or the plots of wicked men, for the Lord is with you; he protects you."

Fortunately, we can grow in wisdom. It is accessible to everyone. In Proverbs 4:8-10, Solomon advised, "If you exalt wisdom, she will exalt you. Hold her fast, and she will lead you to great honor; she will place a beautiful crown upon your head. My son, listen to me and do as I say, and you will have a long, good life."

As chapter 4 closes, we are told above all else to guard our affections. In chapter 5, Solomon warned against sexual sin. He pointed out that after an indiscretion only a bitter conscious remains, sharp as a double-edged sword; she leads you down to death and hell. (see Proverbs 5:4-5)

Chapters 6 through 8 warn against foolish action: "haughtiness, lying, murdering, plotting evil, eagerness to do wrong, a false witness, and sowing discord among brothers." (vv. 16-19) In chapter 9 we learn that wisdom is its own reward: "I, Wisdom, will make the hours of your day more profitable and the years of your life more fruitful." (v.11)

Chapters 10 through 24 cover many topics and thoughtful sayings about the practice of wisdom. Proverbs 10:14 advised, "A wise man holds his tongue. Only a fool blurts out everything he knows; that only leads to sorrow and trouble."

Proverbs 11:2 explained, "Proud men end in shame, but the meek become wise." Solomon spent quite a while talking about the foolishness of pride and conceit. Humility, he reiterated, is a virtue that is paramount to living successfully.

In Proverbs 12:11 we learn, "Hard work means prosperity; only a fool idles away the time." The topic of diligence is central throughout Solomon's writings.

Steven Scott commented, "Diligence is a learnable skill that combines creative persistence, a smart-working effort rightly planned and rightly performed in a timely, efficient, and effective manner to attain a result that is pure and of the highest quality of excellence."8

Diligence will give you ever-increasing success. It will put you in control of a situation, rather than letting the situation control you.

In Proverbs 13:17 we are told, "An unreliable messenger can cause a lot of trouble. Reliable communication permits progress."

Communication skills were another of Solomon's major concerns. What we say and how we say it can have a life-changing impact on others.9 Communication can either escalate anger or extinguish it. We can wound or heal through the power of words. Our mouths can either tear others down or build them up.

Proverbs 14:8 advised, "The wise man looks ahead. The fool attempts to fool himself and won't face facts." Warnings about ignorance and irresponsibility pop up frequently in Solomon's writings. Ignoring the long-term consequences of our actions is dangerous.

Proverbs 15:2 stated, "A wise teacher makes learning a joy; a rebellious teacher spouts foolishness." Solomon taught that effective communication brings material success, joy, fulfillment, and lasting friendships. In Proverbs 16:16 Solomon confided, "How much better is wisdom than gold and understanding than silver."

Solomon wrote often of the foolishness of greed and avarice. He continued in the third verse of the next chapter: "Silver and gold are purified by fire, but God purifies hearts."

Proverbs 18:10 highlighted the paramount importance of revering God: "The Lord is a strong fortress. The godly run to him and are safe." Proverbs 19:2 continued, "It is dangerous and sinful to rush into the unknown."

Proverbs 20:18 warned, "Don't go ahead with your plans without the advice of others; don't go to war until they agree." It is prudent to seek the counsel of mentors.

"He who shuts his ears to the cries of the poor will be ignored in his own time of need."(21:13) In addition to concern for the needy, God is also concerned that young ones receive help and support. In chapter 22, Solomon wrote, "Teach a child to choose the right path and when he is older, he will remain upon it." (v.6) This thought was continued in Proverbs 23: 13, "Don't fail to correct your children; discipline won't hurt them."

Proverbs 24: 13-14 encouraged, "My son, honey whets the appetite and so does wisdom! When you enjoy becoming wise, there is hope for you! A bright future lies ahead!" There are many benefits to choosing a life of obedience and thoughtful action.

Chapters 25 through 28 teach about wisdom for leaders. Chapter 25 counseled, "Be patient and you will finally win, for a soft tongue can break hard bones." (v.15) Patience is the sign of a wise man. A fool does not have sense. Proverbs 26:7 insisted, "In the mouth of a fool a proverb becomes as useless as a paralyzed leg."

Chapter 27:21 conveyed, "The purity of silver and gold can be tested in a crucible, but a man is tested by his reactions to men's praise." Proverbs 28:23 explained, "In the end, people appreciate frankness more than flattery."

Choose truth over undeserved praise, even if that truth comes in the form of criticism. Proverbs 29:1 said, "The man who is often reproved but refuses to accept criticism will suddenly be broken and never have another chance." Garnering wisdom is a serious business. Without wisdom, we will not succeed.

Scott presented the concept of apprenticeship to the God of the Universe. He instructed, "Begin to hold Him in the highest esteem, honor Him as God, and make Him the boss of your life."10

The greatest honor we could give to God and to ourselves is immersion in an intimate, loving and trusting relationship with Him. Walk through your day with an awareness of His presence every step of the way. Pray to Him continually for guidance. He wants to hear your ideas and dreams. He also wants to experience your gratitude for the many gifts He dispenses daily.

In Ecclesiastes 12:13, Solomon explained, "Here now is my final conclusion: Fear God and obey his commands, for this is everyone's duty."

Solomon also used wisdom in writing *Song of Songs*. On a literal level it honored the sanctity of marriage. It represented the purity and sacredness that should surround marital intimacy. On a figurative level it is a brilliant allegory of God's love for Israel and the church.

Solomon's reign is believed to have spanned from c. 976 to 931 BC. He belongs to the Davidic dynasty. Its chronology can be checked against datable Babylonian and Assyrian records.

Solomon's time of governing Israel is associated with the peak golden age of the independent Jewish nation. The Israelite monarchy gained its greatest splendor and wealth during the 40 years he reigned.11

In addition to the temple, Solomon also built several other important structures in Jerusalem. He took 13 years building a royal palace on a hill in central Jerusalem. He constructed great works to secure a supply of water for the city as well as structures for the defense of the city.

Though Solomon was the wisest of the wise, he made some dire mistakes. He had an astounding 700 wives and 300 concubines. He sealed many political alliances by marrying pagan women. He allowed his wives to negate his loyalty to Yahweh.

According to 1 Kings 11:4, Solomon's "wives turned his heart after other gods." They convinced him to build temples to the deities worshipped in the nations from which they originated. This incurred great wrath and retribution from God that led to the division of the kingdom after Solomon's death.

Solomon was wise but fatally flawed. The New Testament ushered in the only perfect man who ever existed. The Gospel accounts tell of the birth, life, and death of God's only begotten Son, Jesus. Although mere humankind had miserably failed, Jesus fulfilled every letter of the law.

God sent Jesus to earth as a human being to help us understand God and His plan for our lives. Matthew 6:20 promises that when we ask Jesus into every aspect of our being, we are building up "treasures in heaven." Treasures in heaven cannot be stolen, destroyed or tarnished by time.12

In Matthew 7:24-27, Jesus explained to His listeners how to live wisely: "All who listen to my instructions and follow them are wise, like a man who builds his house on solid rock. Though the rain comes in torrents and the floodwaters rise and the winds beat against that house, it won't collapse, for it is built on rock. But those who hear my instructions and ignore them are foolish, like a man who builds his house on sand. For when the rains and floods come, and the storm winds beat against his house, it will fall with a mighty crash."

It is astonishing to realize that we can actually develop the mind of Christ. Philippians 2:5 affirmed, "Let this mind be in you which was also in Christ Jesus."

In 1 Corinthians 2:16, Paul asked, "For who has known or understood the mind (the counsels and purposes) of the Lord so as to guide and instruct Him and give Him knowledge? But we have the mind of Christ (the Messiah) and do hold the thoughts (feelings and purposes) of His heart." (AMP) How encouraging!

James 1:5 enlightened us, "If any of you is deficient in wisdom, let him ask of the giving God [Who gives] to everyone liberally and ungrudgingly, without reproaching or faultfinding, and it will be given to him." (AMP)

John Wooden, longtime UCLA basketball coach, was named the greatest coach of the twentieth century by ESPN in 1999. He displayed incredible wisdom in the manner in which he recruited players.

Surprisingly, he was not a man preoccupied with winning. His focus, rather, was on the potential and improvement possible for each of his players.

While most recruiters scoured high school gyms in search of talent and athleticism, Coach Wooden's primary consideration was the student's transcript. To him, a student's discipline said a great deal about that player. Wooden wanted his players' first goal to be to graduate from college.

John Wooden's second criterion was the student's relationship with his family. Did the student treat his parents with respect and his siblings with kindness? The coach knew that these types of relational skills were a necessary part of teamwork and camaraderie.

The third criterion consisted of a composite evaluation by six coaches. He did not want to base his decisions on one game but rather on the player's consistency over time. So he had six experts watch the potential recruit at length.

The coach's final criteria in making player selections were based on the boys' quickness and natural ability. He knew talent was irreplaceable but refused to select a player without seriously deliberating on the player's priorities, relationships, and track record of solid and consistent performance.13

Coach Wooden exhibited great wisdom throughout his coaching career. Solomon was the wisest man who ever lived. Jesus, however, was God Himself. He was the very Creator of wisdom and everything else that exists. He was the greatest Coach of all coaches.

In the last book of the New Testament, Jesus made a wonderful promise. He said, "Behold, I stand at the door and knock. If anyone hears My voice and opens the door, I will come in to him and dine with him, and he with Me." (Revelation 3:20 NKJV)

May we dine with Jesus always. It would be wise. It would be prudent…and it will be magnificent.

4 PEACE: BEING A MARY IN A HEROD-RULED WORLD

"The angel answered, 'The Holy Spirit will come upon you, the power of the Highest hover over you; therefore, the child you bring to birth will be called Holy, Son of God.' …Mary said, 'Yes, I see it all now; I'm the Lord's maid, ready to serve. Let it be with me just as you say.'" (Luke 1: 35, 37 Message)

In our busy, overcommitted lives, we must pause to examine the health of our souls. Are we keeping ourselves in perfect peace, or are we dragging ourselves through an endless, stressful cycle of putting out fires?

Putting out those fires can inflate our pride, but pride can be dangerous. King Herod's life exemplified just how dangerous a situation becomes when a huge ego feels threatened.

On the other hand, Mary, Jesus' mother, epitomized peace. Her quiet manner infused every fiber of her being. She faced challenges humbly and obediently. When we consider how much Mary had to endure in her lifetime, we see her as a deeply inspiring heroine.

If positive psychology is characterized by the study of the truly good life, Mary's story provides a wonderful case study. In *What Happy Women Know*, authors Dan Baker and Cathy Greenburg note, "Happiness is far more than a mood or emotion. It is a way of being, a way of knowing what's right and good, and living true to that."[1]

Certainly Mary had a most graceful and dignified way of living. She reached for God's will in every situation and placed her dependence and trust in Him. Hence, even in the darkest times, Mary's composure was the steady center of her personality.

This chapter is designed to help us tap into our essential peacefulness – a serenity Mary beautifully exemplified. This is a peace that passes all understanding. It is the tranquility necessary to sustain you as you pick up and carry your cross. Your cross is borne as you live out your distinct calling despite the challenges you face.

Like Mary, you are to complete the full purpose of your life on earth. To do that you will need the deep-seated equanimity that only faith in God can give.

It is interesting to note that the United Nations Educational, Scientific, and

Cultural Organization (UNESCO) regards individual and group peace and human rights as essential human strengths.2 This organization characterizes peace as a "dynamic, holistic, and lifelong process through which mutual respect, understanding, caring, sharing, compassion, social responsibility, solidarity, acceptance, and tolerance of diversity among individuals and groups …are internalized…This process begins with the development of inner peace…of individuals engaged in the search for truth, knowledge, and understanding."3

Mary's inner peace was so deep and reflexive that she could accept a visit from the angel Gabriel without missing a beat. Gabriel told Mary that she was highly favored in God's eyes. He then proclaimed to her that she would bear God's Son, the Savior of the world.

Try to put yourself in Mary's situation. What would your first thoughts have been on receiving such news? Would you feel dumbfounded by the fact that God had decided to use you in such an astounding way? Would you marvel that, though you were a virgin, God would conceive a baby in your womb? Would you be terrified that your fiancé would never understand something so incomprehensible? What emotions might you have in such a situation? Would fear, doubt, disbelief, and lack of comprehension be just a few of your feelings?

Yet look at Mary's first utterance upon receiving such life altering news: "I am the Lord's servant, and I am willing to do whatever he wants. May everything you said come true." (Luke 1:38) Notice the feminine acquiescence. As quickly as Gabriel cast this reality on her, she moved into harmony with God's will. Her focus was not on her own well-being or the sacrifices she would have to make. Rather, she was pliant and willing to do whatever the Lord directed her to do. In fact, she was inspired to sing; "For he, the mighty Holy One, has done great things to me." (Luke 4:9) What a lovely response.

Mary displayed her inner beauty, strength, and abiding tranquility. Certainly, she must have wondered how her betrothed would accept all this. Fortunately, an angelic messenger appeared to Joseph and explained the reality of the situation. Joseph responded by making Mary his wife.

Another challenge arrived – tax time. An almost-due Mary rode atop a donkey from Nazareth all the way to Bethlehem. Once again, our heroine maintained her calm in the midst of discomfort. She and Joseph finally arrived in town only to discover there was no vacancy at the inn. They took shelter in a stable, where Jesus was born. Gently, they placed Him in a manger. Not exactly an ideal environment! Still, Mary maintained her serenity.

Soon shepherds entered the stable and disclosed an amazing story. Angels had appeared to them as they were tending their sheep. Accompanied by a multitude of angels, one angel of the Lord announced that the Messiah had entered the world.

Surely those shepherds were elated. However, the new mother "quietly treasured these things in her heart and often thought about them." (Luke 2:19)

Mary's countenance must have glowed. She had her beautiful, perfect child - Jesus. Twelve years later, though, she temporarily lost Him at a festival. After a frantic search, she found Him in the temple, where He was conversing wisely with the Jewish elders.

When Jesus was an adult, Mary told Him the wedding they were attending had run out of wine. In response, He turned water into wine. What joy she must have experienced at that festive celebration as He performed His first miracle.

But Mary experienced great sorrow at the end of Jesus' ministry. From the foot of His cross, she watched Him experience an agonizing death. She saw the blood running down His face from His crown of thorns. She heard His gasps for breath and His cries of anguish. She was there the moment God turned His face away from His son as Jesus took the sins of the world upon Himself. He hung there before His mother and endured His shame and degradation.

Mary did not scream. She did not shatter. Her heart was fully breaking within her and yet – even then – she accepted God's will. She submitted herself to the nightmare – and she endured. Her thoughts were not focused on herself. There was no self-pity in her expression. She held strong to the belief that God had a larger plan and purpose in her Son's suffering.

She chose to trust. She made a decision to abide in peace. In deference and faith, she turned everything in her soul over to her Lord. Amid the desperation of the moment, she maintained her stability. Is it any wonder that God chose her to be the most blessed among all women?

Paul's words in Philippians 4:6-7 reflect the way Mary conducted herself: "Be anxious for nothing, but in everything by prayer and supplication, with thanksgiving, let your requests be made known to God. And the peace of God, which surpasses all understanding, will guard your hearts and minds through Christ Jesus." (NKJV)

What does Mary's life teach you about the challenges you are currently facing in your life? What can you take away from her deep composure? Can you move beyond mere survival when faced with overwhelmingly difficult life issues? Can you empower yourself to meet them in such a way that you become a role model as Mary was? There are many ways to thrive. Peter thrived boldly. Mary thrived with quiet dignity.

Susan, a retired schoolteacher, lost her son to suicide. How do you overcome something so devastating? It is very painful, but day after day, Susan puts her son's soul in God's hands. She plants marigolds at her son's grave and believes she will see him again someday. She lives out her heartache with the same quiet dignity Mary displayed while enduring Jesus' suffering on the cross.

Juxtapose such dignity and integrity with the actions of a man driven and obsessed with power – the infamous King Herod. There was nothing peaceful about him.

The wise men arrived in Jerusalem in search of the infant Jesus, the King of the Jews. They asked Herod where they could find Him. Their inquiry deeply disturbed King Herod. He attempted to gather more information about this child's whereabouts. He considered the infant a direct threat to his throne. He was incensed when, after worshiping baby Jesus, the wise men took an alternate route home to avoid giving Herod any information.

Herod's paranoia continued to mount. He vowed to kill every male under two years old in the town and surrounding countryside to make sure he destroyed the King of the Jews. However, an angel foiled Herod's plan by appearing to Joseph, telling him to flee to Egypt with Mary and Jesus. They lived there safely until King Herod died.

Herod was controlled by greed. Power and possessions, his paramount values, gave him his inflated position and identity. He allowed things that had no eternal value to consume him. He built his house upon the sand instead of on the rock.

Herod did not blink when he ordered the slaughter of all those innocent male babies. He did not hesitate to destroy anyone he perceived to be a threat. Being extremely insecure and suspicious, he felt himself to be literally surrounded by such threats.

King Herod's paranoia became a self-fulfilling prophecy. His ugly jealousy created a life of ineffectiveness, failure, and evil. He was inflamed with imaginary fears that eventually swallowed him whole.

One Tin Soldier Rides Away is a song from the 1970's about a group of people who had a treasure that another group wanted. The group with the treasure suggested they dig up the treasure together and share it, but the other group was greedy and ruthlessly slaughtered the group that had the treasure on their property. After everyone from the group who had the treasure was dead and out of the way, the warring group dug up the treasure. The treasure was simply a rock – "peace on earth was all it said."

James 3:16 explains: "For wherever there is jealousy (envy) and contention (rivalry and selfish ambition) there will also be confusion (unrest, disharmony, rebellion) and all sorts of evil and vile practices." (AMP)

Misguided King Herod blatantly failed to acknowledge the truth that ultimately it is God and God alone who is in control. In his hubris, Herod refused to submit to God's will for his life. Peace does not come from forcing others to bow down before us, but rather from choosing to bow down humbly before the omnipotent Creator of the universe.

If we persist in refusing to trust God, we will be plagued with fear and anguish. We can only live in victory if we allow our lives to be clay in the Potter's hands. There is only one Potter. Having the audacity to "play god" in an attempt to control others always causes insecurity and hostility. It leads inevitably to failure and destruction.

Throughout his manipulations and machinations, Herod refused to seek the one element he needed most of all – inner peace. It is not by winning contests or conquests that we find meaning in life. We can achieve peace through admitting our sins and our great need for God's involvement in every aspect of our lives. It is in crying out for help to our Father, our Abba, that healing and restoration occur.

Poor Herod – he never got it. He never understood the essential truth of life or came to any comprehension about what really leads to a meaningful and satisfying existence. He never took comfort in the Lord the way we can. Isaiah 54:10 declared: "For though the mountains should depart and the hills be shaken or removed, yet My love and kindness shall not depart from you, nor shall My covenant of peace and completeness removed, says the Lord, Who has compassion on you." (AMP)

For further reassurance, jump forward a few chapters to Isaiah 66: 12-13: "For thus says the Lord: 'Behold, I will extend peace to her (Jerusalem) like a river, and the glory of the Gentiles like a flowing stream. Then you (true worshipers and their offspring) shall feed; on her sides shall you be carried, and be dandled on her knees, as one whom his mother comforts, so I will comfort you; and you shall be comforted in Jerusalem.'" (NKJV)

It is no coincidence that the image of the mother is often synonymous with peace. These images of the comforting mother in the Old Testament foreshadow the great compassion and peacefulness of Jesus' mother.

How can we, like Mary, conduct our lives with dignity and equanimity? Philippians 4:8 gives us clues: "Finally, brethren, whatsoever things are true, whatsoever things are honest, whatsoever things are just, whatsoever things are pure, whatsoever things are lovely, whatsoever things are of good report; If there be any virtue, and if there be any praise, think on these things." (KJV)

These are beautiful sentiments and would indeed be an ideal way to think and live. However, we cannot will ourselves to be good. On our own we are weak and ineffectual creatures. In our own power we will never be adequate. We have to look to and cling to Jesus to provide for all our needs and problems.

In John 14:27 Jesus promised, "I am leaving you with a gift – peace of mind and heart! And the peace I give isn't fragile like the peace the world gives. So don't be troubled or afraid."

Jesus' peace, mirroring his mother's serene nature, fulfills and satisfies our deepest longings. When we trust in and rest in the arms of Christ, we will flourish and find lasting and impenetrable harmony with Him.

Take time to examine your specific strengths and talents. Think about your strongest aptitudes. Are you willing to have an attitude that exhibits peace and stillness as you fulfill your unique calling? Are you grafted into an interdependent community of fellows to which you are able to give and receive security and steadiness?

Leo the Great, who was pope from September 29, 440, to November 10, 461, once said, "Peace is the first thing the angels sang. Peace is the mark of the sons of God. Peace is the nurse of love. Peace is the mother of unity. Peace is the rest of blessed souls. Peace is the dwelling place of eternity."[4]

Peace grows when people use self-control and wisdom in the way they conduct their lives. The great gift of peace arrives when such people have straightened out their priorities. When we truly think about what is important and what matter most, it has little to do with putting our fires or rushing from one mindless activity to another.

We can pause, slow down, and get in tune with the music of God's soul. When we do this, we, like Mary, will be able to endure even the toughest of challenges.

5 ENTHUSIASM AND COMMITMENT: WITH ALL HIS HEART, WITH ALL YOUR HEART

"When Jesus arrived in the villages of Caesarea Philippi, he asked his disciples, 'What are people saying about who the Son of Man is?...And how about you? Who do you say I am?' Simon Peter said, 'You're the Christ, the Messiah, the Son of the Living God.' Jesus came back, 'God bless you, Simon ..My Father in heaven, God himself, let you in on this secret of who I really am…You are Peter, a rock. This is the rock on which I will put together My church, a church so expansive with energy that not even the gates of hell will be able to keep it out.'" (Matthew 16: 13-18 Message)

Giving your life over to Christ will lead you on an adventure more wonderful than your wildest dreams! Throw away your excuses and your fears. Let go of hurts. Let Jesus heal your wounds and wipe away your tears, and then reach for all Christ has to give you. If you do this with enthusiasm and commitment, your life will take on a new energy. Deep inside you lies a passion only Christ can ignite.

Simon Peter had just such a passion. His heart's desire was to magnify Christ and lead others to the Savior. By examining his life, we will be able to see that from his initial brashness and impulsivity as a crusty fisherman, he was refined through his experiences with Christ into a man of vitality and dedication. Peter means "rock." Throughout his time with Jesus, Peter the "rock" became more and more polished.

The chief character strengths Peter exhibited throughout his lifetime were commitment and enthusiasm. Perhaps we can take away a little something from Peter's life that would improve our own walk with God. You and I can study Peter to find out how to be a foundation on which Christ will build His church.

We can also learn from Peter's character strengths of enthusiasm and commitment that it is OK to fail and try again. Seeing the humanness of his many foibles, we will be encouraged that we, too, can be cultivated under God's healing touch.

If we, like Peter, try to walk on the water to Jesus, Jesus will extend a hand to help us. We must try and keep on trying to connect with God. It is always worthwhile to abandon our human perspective to embrace God's total omniscience. On our own, we creep along the ground. Upon discovering the indwelling of Christ, we soar.

How do we connect with God and learn to soar? It is through regular study of God's Word, which is alive and active. Prayer is vital, as is gathering with other believers. Doing things for others is beneficial. However, if we are to truly transcend our limitations, we must take up our cross with all the enthusiasm and commitment we can muster.

Ponder how completing your daily tasks contributes to a larger purpose. God-given goals can lead you on your way. "For goals to be effective, people must be committed to them," says Edwin Locke in the *Handbook of Positive Psychology*. "This is especially critical when goals are difficult and thus require considerable thinking and effort. Action is the ultimate proof of commitment. After all, people can say they are committed and not really mean it. Two types of causal factors are critical in commitment: the belief that the goal is important and the belief that one can achieve or make progress toward it. For a goal to be important it must be tied to an important value."[1]

Surely sharing the saving grace of salvation is a worthy value. Will you commit yourself here and now to the goal of furthering God's kingdom? The narrow road will not always be the easy one to walk; but by taking one step at a time on that walk, you are taking action that can change your life and the lives of others for eternity. This goal is of utmost importance. With the Holy Spirit's help, you can make significant progress toward helping gather Christ's flock for the day of redemption.

We can check our hearts and see if we are experiencing the deep satisfaction of discovering and carrying out our individual roles in the grander scheme of things. Every one of us needs purpose in our lives. God will joyfully bestow that purpose on you if you will only ask.

Peter became increasingly aligned with his purpose. He used his strengths and talents to bring others to Christ. He pursued his goals with great zest.

What are your specific strengths and talents? Are you using your aptitudes to the maximum degree for God's glory and the redemption of those who are still lost? What attitudes are you displaying? Are you exhibiting zest as you fulfill your unique calling?

Living zestfully means "approaching life with excitement and energy; not doing things halfway or halfheartedly; living life as an adventure; feeling alive and activated."[2] You can make living zestfully contagious by sharing your commitment and enthusiasm with others in the body of Christ.

Are you grafted into an interdependent community of fellows where you are able to give and receive support for the journey? Jesus Himself enjoyed the fellowship of His twelve disciples. Hopefully when we are in our Garden of Gethsemane, our entire support system won't abandon us in favor of a nap as Jesus' disciples did while He was praying earnestly to God for strength to endure what He was about to suffer.

While Jesus fervently prayed right before His time of crucifixion for the bitter cup of the cross to be taken from Him, His closest friends slept. Don't you think looking back that those disciples wished they had shown more commitment and enthusiasm in praying for their Master?

I have a friend whose husband was in a head-on collision with a dump truck one icy morning several years ago. Throughout her husband's months of rehabilitation and recovery, she was a solid rock. She slept every night in the waiting room on an air mattress. As a magazine's editor-in-chief, she kept up with her work from a laptop in that same waiting room for many long weeks.

Her tenacity was tested one night when the nursing staff was shorthanded and her husband was running a terribly high fever. They put him on a bed of ice. My friend had to cool him down by placing wet washcloths on him the entire night.

What does Peter's life have to say to you about the challenges you currently face in your life? How can you learn from his example? Can you see how Peter was able to thrive despite the mistakes and failures in his life? Do you have the inner strength to do likewise?

Jesus called Peter a rock because of his unswerving devotion. I saw my friend act with such strong commitment and unfailing love toward her husband in a time of crisis that I knew Jesus was shining through her.

Peter made many mistakes. But he always let Jesus shine through him. Fortunately, God does not demand perfection. Peter truly loved God with a zestful heart though he often let Jesus and himself down. So, too, we often let Him and ourselves down.

Ponder for a moment the occasions when Peter disappointed Jesus. When Jesus told His disciples what He would suffer, Peter fought it. Jesus had to say to him, "Get behind Me, Satan."

Think about the time Jesus told Peter he would deny knowing Christ three times before the cock crowed. Peter swore vehemently that he would never forsake Jesus. But within hours he did deny Jesus three times.

Can you imagine how Peter felt at that moment the cock crowed? I certainly remember occasions in my own life when I recognized what a horrible sinner I was. Don't you imagine Peter probably felt he had completely failed in his mission - that he had utterly ruined his relationship with the Lord? However, this is not where the story ends.

After His resurrection, Jesus appeared to the disciples on the shore. They had returned to fishing. At a wonderful morning meal Jesus had prepared, Jesus asked Peter three times: Do you love Me? Three times Peter emphatically answered he did. Three times Jesus told him to feed His little lambs.

So Peter's denial was not the end of his relationship with Jesus. I sometimes think Jesus asked Peter three times about his allegiance to actually heal and help Peter overcome the three times he had denied Him.

Notice how Jesus focused on Peter's strengths rather than his weaknesses. Likewise, Martin Seligman, speaking about positive psychology, explained, "I do not believe that you should devote overly much effort to correcting your weaknesses. Rather, I believe that the highest success in living and the deep emotional satisfaction comes from building and using your signature strengths."3

So Christ Himself told Peter he had an extremely important mission and it was to be so. Jesus instructed His apostles to go and make disciples of all the nations, baptizing them and teaching them to obey God's commandments. This is the Great Commission. As it was for Peter, it is our commission too.

Jesus promised never to leave His disciples, and He is speaking to us also. We have been given the Holy Spirit who comforts, counsels, and directs us if only we will hearken an ear to His still, small voice.

Well, guess what Peter ended up spearheading? On the Day of Pentecost, the Holy Spirit descended on Peter and the other believers. Peter preached to the crowd of Jews assembled for the Feast of Pentecost. He explained what was happening by reading prophesy from the book of Joel: "In the last days, God said, 'I will pour out my Holy Spirit upon all mankind, and your sons and daughters shall prophesy, and your young men shall see visions, and your old men will dream dreams'." (Acts 2:17)

Pretty good preaching for a burly, unschooled fisherman, wouldn't you say? This is what Christ's presence in a life can do – and it is as true for you and me as it was for Peter.

After Peter's sermon, the crowd called out, asking what they should do. According to Acts 2:38 Peter instructed them to turn from sin, return to God, and be baptized in the name of Jesus Christ for the forgiveness of their sins. Those who did this received the gift of the Holy Spirit. At this point about three thousand people were baptized.

Soon after this, Peter performed miracles and preached persuasively to fulfill the Great Commission. The authorities began to watch Peter closely. It was confounding to them how two uneducated and nonprofessional men such as Peter and John had grown so confident and well-spoken since being with Jesus.

The Council of High Priests was intimidated, and told Peter and John to be silent. However, these two bold apostles refused to stop talking about all that had happened to them since following Jesus. May you and I be so enthused and committed. May we never stop telling others all the wonderful things that have happened to us since we began to follow Jesus. This is the path to increased spiritual growth and personal success.

Peter's enthusiasm and commitment were unstoppable. He and the other apostles healed many. The sick actually vied for a position on the road just so Peter's shadow would fall across them as he went by. He restored to health all the sick and demon-possessed he encountered. That was the power of the complete faith Peter had in Jesus.

In Acts 10, Peter was meditating on a flat rooftop. He had a vision in which the sky opened and a great sheet settled on the ground. In the sheet were all types of animals that God had forbidden the Jews to eat. God told Peter to kill and eat any of them. Headstrong Peter refused. He retorted that he had never done such a thing. God replied that, if He said something was kosher, then it truly was. This vision challenging Peter's view on what was clean or unclean repeated three times.

Peter was perplexed. God was changing the rules and it was scary to leave known territory. Can you relate? The uncertainty of trying to follow God's will is only possible if we relinquish our ideas of how we think things ought to go. Throughout this confusing time, God was preparing Peter for his next great endeavor: to bring the Good News to the Gentiles.

God showed Peter that he should never think of anyone as inferior. Do an inventory of your prejudices. Is there anyone in God's creation to whom you secretly think you are superior? Peter, the proud man of Jewish ancestry, had to rethink his basic paradigms. He had to think on his feet, for he was going to be the vessel through which God would bring together people who had been separated by huge barriers. In Acts 10:34 Peter exclaimed, "I see very clearly that the Jews are not God's only favorites."

After this, when Peter began ministering to the Gentiles, the Holy Spirit fell upon those who believed. The Jewish leaders, however, were unhappy with what Peter was doing. They began to plot against him. They often imprisoned him for his preaching. Would you have the devotion to speak the Word of Christ if it meant you would suffer greatly as a result? We never really know what we would do in such a situation, but it is worth pondering.

One night while Peter was in jail, an angel came to him and released him. The angel escorted him out of prison and opened each locked door they encountered. Amy Grant wrote a song about this – *Angels watching over me, every step I take.*

Peter, the rough fisherman, went on to write two epistles. At the time, around A.D. 64, Christians were being martyred for believing in Jesus Christ. Peter's first letter was written to encourage suffering Jewish Christians. In this writing, Peter passed on the shepherd's crook to the elders of the new Christian movement by saying, "Shepherd the flock of God which is among you, serve as overseers, not by compulsion but willingly, not for dishonest gain but eagerly; not as being lords over those entrusted to you, but being examples to the flock; and when the Chief Shepherd appears, you will receive the crown of glory that does not fade away." (1 Peter 5: 2-4 NKJV)

Do you notice the parallel between Peter's admonition to the elders to shepherd the flock and Jesus' earlier injunction to Peter to "feed My sheep"? He did this, as always, with characteristic fervor. May we learn from his example how the fruits of enthusiasm and commitment can change the world.

Second Peter was written around A.D. 66-67. By this time Peter's message had expanded from Jewish Christians to all believers everywhere. As he wrote, Peter was not expecting to see his readers again. His words were meant to embolden the believers to be faithful to God and to warn them to watch out against false teachings. This second epistle opens with Peter's advice on how to grow spiritually:

"Giving all diligence, add to your faith virtue, to virtue knowledge, to knowledge self-control, to self-control perseverance, to perseverance godliness, to godliness brotherly kindness, and to brotherly kindness love. For if these things are yours and abound, you will be neither barren nor unfruitful in the knowledge of our Lord Jesus Christ." (2 Peter 1: 4-8 NKJV)

What about you? What is your heart telling you to do? How are you to bear fruit in your situation with your unique gifts and talents?

Think of the marvelous enthusiasm Billy Graham has shown over the course of his lifetime. He has made it his mission to present the Good News to as many people as possible. He lives out his mission joyfully, skillfully, and faithfully.

Over the years, as Billy circled the globe to share the Good News, his wife, Ruth, stayed at home and raised their five children. Billy later commented that because he was called away so often, Ruth became both mother and father to their children. Yet she never complained or asked him to stay home. She was brimming over with commitment to her husband, and significantly, she was filled with dedication to the Lord.

Our strengths and talents shine brightly through the broken jar of clay that is our identity. Peter was just such an imperfect vessel. God can use us in our humanness to accomplish important things. We must, like Peter, let go of fear and hold onto faith. When we trust God in an enthusiastic and committed manner, God can do great things with our lives.

We should desire above all else to further Christ's Kingdom. Living to accomplish God's purposes is the most exciting endeavor that can be experienced.

You can serve the Lord each day with great enthusiasm and commitment. Just surrender your life over to Him. Surely it is the truth to say that Peter served the Lord with his whole heart. Will you follow Peter's example?

6 GRATITUDE: MARY MAGDALENE WASHES FEET AND THE CLEANSED LEPER GIVES THANKS

"Do you see this woman? I came to your home: you provided no water for my feet, but she rained tears on my feet and dried them with her hair. You gave me no greeting, bur from the time I arrived she hasn't quit kissing my feet. You provided nothing for freshening up, but she has soothed my feet with perfume. Impressive, isn't it? She was forgiven many, many sins, and so she is very, very grateful." (Luke 7: 44-46 Message)

Sometimes we become so bogged down in our trials that we forget to express gratitude. However, it is those very trials that help us grow and mature. As we look back over our lives with the perspective that only time allows, we can see that in accepting our hardships, we became more loving, more patient, and kinder.

Have you ever heard the expression "a Kodak moment"? This is a memory we want to cherish forever. Sometimes we have a camera handy. Sometimes just experiencing the moment's beauty through the windows of our minds is the perfect response. We can hold those memories close to our heart always.

When we get to the end of our adventure on planet Earth, we will see how each step of the way led us closer to our desired destination. We will see how Jesus was there with us at every step, and we will be grateful.

Whatever challenges you are facing today, remember this: a negative attitude is the only true disability. We are enabled when we choose to think positively about our lives. When we spiral downward into negativity, we become disabled.

Emmit Miller, A TV news anchor in California, once said, "Gratitude has to do with feeling full, complete, adequate – we have everything we need and deserve, we approach the world with a sense of value."[1]

Luke 7 focuses on a prostitute strong enough to value herself. She knew her sins were many, but she also knew Christ could forgive her. What a tender, intimate moment in Jesus' life Luke revealed to us!

Notice Jesus' response to the repentant woman. The Lord derives much pleasure from a sincere offering of gratitude.

In Leviticus, we learn that in ancient times the fat from the sacrificial animal was considered the choicest part of the offering. Symbolically this helps us remember that God deserves the very best from us. He wants us to commit our lives to Him completely, believing it is worth the cost.

We see that this woman discussed in Luke gave everything she had – body, mind, and soul – in overflowing appreciation for Jesus and His boundless mercy. Jesus responded to the pure gratitude of a fallen prostitute by completely forgiving and restoring her. Will He do any less for you and me if we sincerely repent?

Sometimes the way we live displeases and dishonors the Lord and disrupts our fellowship with Him. But when we make all-out heartfelt offerings of gratitude to Him, He reconciles with us and rescues us from ourselves. Our offering of thanksgiving, like the prostitute's, shows God we appreciate His blessings, healing, and help in difficult times.

Gratitude has a way of giving us eyes to see all of life as a gift. It is a key element for sparking positive changes in individuals, families, and organizations.2

Just as Mary Magdalene's act of adoration toward Jesus had a rippling effect throughout the community, so our gratitude affects those around us. Can't you just imagine that the disciples and town folk spent many a speculative conversation trying to understand this surprising mystery of the love expressed between Mary Magdalene and Jesus?

At the end of the story, Jesus told the (now former) prostitute that her faith had saved her. Then He told her to go and enter into peace. The Hebrew word for peace is *shalom*. It is a rich term that encompasses the concepts of vibrant physical heath, robust emotional wellbeing, bounteous material prosperity, and ethereal spiritual wholeness.

An act of wholehearted praise – as this woman made by bathing Jesus' feet in her perfumed hair – can restore completeness and harmony to the penitent's life. The people that God blankets with love do not necessarily have wonderful past records. He can give people who have made deeply scarring mistakes, such as Mary Magdalene, a blessed and power-filled future.

Wouldn't you treasure the opportunity to wash Jesus' feet with costly perfume? Do you know you can spend your day in such a way that it is a sweet aroma lifted to the Lord? How would you spend such a day?

What if you had been at the Last Supper? What if you had been given the experience of having Jesus wash your feet?

It has been said that demons feed on the dust of the feet. What dust remains on your feet from roads you have walked? Would you be willing to ask Jesus to wash all the dust off your feet and make you clean? What past events in your life need to be cleansed of dust? Keep your feet "dust-free" through prayer, forgiveness, confession of your sins, and praise.

It means a lot when we, like Mary Magdalene, choose to praise Him in a public forum. When we make our thanks visible to others we grow spiritually and can be an example for others to follow. The seventh chapter of Leviticus confirms that God wants us to honor Him publicly.

Leviticus 7: 1-5 instructed, "These are the instructions for the guilt offering. It is most holy. The animal sacrifice as a guilt offering must be slaughtered at the place where the burnt offerings are slaughtered, and its blood must be splattered against all sides of the altar. The priest will then offer all its fat on the altar, including the fat of the broad tail, the fat around the internal organs, the two kidneys and the fat around them near the loins, and the long lobe of the liver. These are to be removed with the kidneys, and the priests will burn them on the altar as a special gift presented to the LORD. This is the guilt offering."

David was never bashful about being demonstrative about his God. He wrote many "thank you" letters to Him in the Psalms. In Psalm 92: 1-4, he said, "It is a good and delightful thing to give thanks to the Lord, to sing praises [with musical accompaniment] to Your name, O Most High. To show forth Your loving-kindness in the morning and Your faithfulness by night, with an instrument of ten strings and with the lute, with a solemn sound upon the lyre. For You, O Lord, have made me glad by Your works; at the deeds of Your hands I joyfully sing." (AMP)

The act of praise brings honor to God. It also helps us feel positive about ourselves and our lives. Endorphins are released when we show praise because it feels good to think about what is right with us and our world. It makes for a happy and satisfied life. Praising the Lord will always bring joy and contentedness. This is especially true when God has done something extraordinary in our lives. Particularly if we have been an outcast, perhaps for many years, His acceptance can overwhelm us with the wonder of redemption.

Let's look at another example of Jesus' graciousness when thanksgiving was offered: "And as He was going into one village, He was met by ten lepers, who stood at a distance. And they raised up their voices and called, 'Jesus, Master, take pity and have mercy on us!' And when He saw them, He said to them, 'Go [at once] and show yourselves to the priests.' And as they went, they were cured and made clean. Then one of them, upon seeing that he was cured, turned back, recognizing and thanking and praising God with a loud voice; And he fell prostrate at Jesus' feet, thanking Him [over and over.] And he was a Samaritan. Then Jesus asked, 'Were not [all] ten cleansed? Where are the nine? Was there no one found to return and to recognize and give thanks and praise God except this alien?'

"And He said to him, 'Get up and go on your way. Your faith (your trust and confidence that spring from Your belief in God) has restored you to health.'" (Luke 17: 12-19, AMP)

Think of it – ten lepers were healed, but only one came back to thank Jesus. As we think of all God has done for us, let us always remember to go to Jesus and thank Him for His kindness and mercy.

Some strong similarities are apparent between the forgiven prostitute and the newly cleansed leper. Both were of a socially unacceptable caste. Both felt a deep need to show their appreciation to Jesus. They both fell prostrate at His feet, thanking Him repeatedly. Each of their expressions of thanks was wholehearted, deeply passionate, and public.

Jesus sent the former leper on his way, telling him that his faith had restored his health. Similarly, He told the prostitute that her faith had led to the great peace she would experience the rest of her life.

Gratitude changes people. It creates a proactive energy that can move us to a higher, deeper level of living. Giving thanks is an art. It can be cultivated. It brings with it the ability to give and receive joy every day. It is living with an open heart.

My friend Anna has an attitude of gratitude. She suffers from bipolar disorder. She has a very difficult time getting her medications regulated and hence experiences a lot of discomfort and anxiety. Her thoughts frighten her sometimes and she struggles with tears and pain. She has a problem called rumination in which she continues to think and obsess about her past.

Anna is working hard in therapy to rid herself of self-defeating beliefs but it is excruciating work at times. Still, no matter how sick or unsteady she feels, Anna never forgets all the things for which she is grateful. In fact, every night she writes out three things that happened that day for which she is thankful. She is displaying the strength of gratitude in the midst of her suffering.

The Lakota Indian's daily prayer gives us a great example: "Let us give thanks for this beautiful day. Let us give thanks for this life. Let us give thanks for the water without which life would not be possible. Let us give thanks for grandmother earth who protects and nourishes us."

It is so easy to lose sight of how much we have to be grateful for. Notice the thankfulness of the Native American prayer expresses for very simple and basic things – things necessary for life.

Think about something as basic as clean water. Much of the world lacks this most central element for health and survival. As we ponder how wealthy and materially blessed we are compared to most people in other parts of the world, we should feel moved to help. We need to be grateful for every resource we have while simultaneously taking steps to set up systems to help those less fortunate.

Is gratitude one of your strengths? Do you feel you have much to be thankful for? If you wrote a gratitude list, how long would it be? Can you appreciate the situations and relationships that have made up your past? Can you express gratitude simply to give glory to God?

If you aren't as grateful as you think you should be, remember that we are promised in Romans that we can be transformed by the renewal of our minds. We have the ability to learn and change.

Perhaps all of us, to some degree, are saddled with at least a few ingrained negative responses we may have formed in early childhood. In the process of growing up, we all experienced emotional wounding that was hurtful and hard to understand. It is only when we fully realize the depth and breadth of God's love for us that we can heal and grow beyond our hurts. We can change the way we think and so change our experiences. We have the responsibility to create a robust and mature adulthood. We must seek out and integrate attributes such as hope, joy, and yes, gratitude.

We are here on earth "to grow our souls, to heal our wounds – or at least bless our woundedness – and become more loving, kind, fearless, and hopeful," Emmit Miller said.3

It is impossible to feel both the positive emotion of thankfulness and a negative emotion, such as anger or fear, at the same time. When focusing on the positive, fear, anger, and bitterness melt away. Learning to "let go of the struggle" is an amazing feat. It usually happens a little at a time.

God is love personified. He forgets every transgression I have made once I have repented. Through the repentance process, I become lighter and lighter. What I mean is, I lighten up. Joy is mine because what Jesus has done for me buoys me.

Certainly, I am endlessly grateful for the salvation He gave me. I am also immensely grateful for the freedom from bondage He gives me while I am here on earth.

My personal experience with suffering gradually transformed me from an unhappy person to a very grateful one. I'm so thankful that we can progress beyond our ignorance and become wise, disciplined people. This, too, is a process.

It happens when we immerse ourselves in the Word. Gratitude deepens when we ponder His ways. I have a long way to go, but I make it a habit to pause and think of God (Selah). I find that with practice and humility, I can increase the amount of time I am thinking of Him and His precepts.

We are instructed in Philippians 4:8 to think on what is good and pure and edifying. Study the Word diligently. We are forgiven. We are restored. The One who made us loves us deeply and completely. Surely these are great reasons to be grateful.

The following message was found as graffiti on a wall in Berkeley, California: "Gratitude makes us feel good. Mental sunshine will cause the flowers of peace, happiness, and prosperity to grow upon the face of the earth. Be a creator of mental sunshine."

The practice of gratitude is far reaching. When we are grateful, it rubs off on other people. When we feel free and joyful, we can help others frame their lives and experiences in a new and more positive way. We can plant flowers of peace, happiness, and prosperity in the hearts of others. This will help some and rescue many. If people see that we can have robust lives, they will believe they can also.

Gratitude serves as an important antidote to stress, which is rampant in our culture today. Positive feelings can actually release endorphins throughout the body. Thanksgiving can lead us to greater health.

Gratitude opens up our hearts so we can receive all of the good God waits to give us. It is a new way of looking at things and a new way of perceiving that can lead to enhanced well-being.

If we live deeply and authentically long enough, gratitude, like any spiritual practice, can become second nature. Meister Eckhart said, "If the only prayer you say in your whole life is 'thank you' that would suffice."[4]

So often our prayers are requests. We ask for help. We ask for favor. We ask for miracles.

However, if we are unable to see the beauty and grace that is already all around us, how can we expect to be able to receive anything else? Do we spend time just thanking and praising God for all He is doing in our lives? Developing the aptitude of being grateful is a key to personal and spiritual growth.

Personally, we are certainly more eager to help people who show gratitude for what we have done for them. Don't you imagine that God feels the same way? Why would He bless us with more if we do not appreciate all He has already done for us? God must love an attitude of gratitude.

In *Attitudes of Successful Learners*, motivational speaker Chris Widener shared that choosing the right attitude will change the world around you. Widener suggested four attitudes that successful learners possess:

"I can."

"This is a long-term approach."

"Learning is valuable."

"I will make a difference in the lives of those around me."[5]

Gratitude is graceful. It is a mysterious and powerful tool that can open our eyes to see that which we could not see before. The Ojibway have a beautiful saying, "Sometimes I go about with pity for myself and all the while the Great Winds are carrying me across the sky."

"In the history of ideas, gratitude has had surprisingly few detractors," say Bono, Emmons, and McCullough in *Positive Psychology in Practice*. "Nearly every thinker has viewed gratitude as a sentiment with virtually no down side…But the fact that people typically consider gratitude a virtue and not simply a pleasure also points to the fact it does not always come naturally or easily. Gratitude must and can, be cultivated. And by cultivating the virtue, it appears that people may get the pleasure of gratitude, and all of its other attendant benefits, thrown in for free."[6]

Oh, what a blessing the grateful life can be. It connects us with the vast, fierce vibrancy of the universe and it's Maker. Let us say with David in Psalm 116: 16-17, "O, Lord, You have freed me from my bonds, and I will serve You forever. I will worship You and offer You a sacrifice of thanksgiving."

7 HAPPINESS: FOUND ON A ROAD AND UP A TREE

"We pray that you'll live well for the Master, making him proud of you as you work hard in his orchard. As you learn more and more how God works, you will learn how to do your work. We pray that you'll have the strength to stick it out over the long haul – not the grim strength of gritting your teeth but the glory-strength God gives. It is the strength that endures the unendurable and spills over into joy, thanking the Father who makes us strong enough to take part in everything bright and beautiful that he has for us." (Colossians 1: 10-12 Message).

As we look at Bible characters, we see that their lives were grand adventures. Your life, too, can be a grand adventure if you let Jesus take control of it.

By studying the Word, you will be able to step out of fear and guilt and live in the happiness of communion with the Lord. No matter what type of situation you find yourself in today, no matter how paralyzed, embittered, or scarred you are, Jesus can lift you out of your troubles and bring you into a new life.

As positive psychologist Martin Seligman put it, "The good life is using your signature strengths every day to produce authentic happiness and abundant gratification."[1]

In his seminal work, *Authentic Happiness,* Seligman talked about researcher Barbara Fredrickson's concept of broadening and building. The basic idea is that developing more positive emotion builds friendship, love, greater health, and more powerful achievement. He commented, "Barbara Fredrickson's theory and all these studies utterly convinced me that it was worth trying hard to put more positive emotion into my life…broadening and building – that is, growth and positive development – are essential characteristics of a win-win encounter."[2]

He continued, "Fredrickson claims that positive emotions have a grand purpose…They broaden our abiding intellectual, physical, and social resources, building up reserves we can draw upon when a threat or opportunity presents itself. When we are in a positive mood, people like us better, and friendship, love, and coalitions are more likely to cement. In contrast to the constrictions of negative emotion, our mental set is expansive, tolerant, and creative. We are open to new ideas and new experiences."3

Creating happy experiences is good for us. As Christians we need to aspire to and practice thinking positively. Seligman commented, "It turns out that adults and children who are put into a good mood select higher goals, perform better, and persist longer."4

To live in a consistently productive state is a worthy pursuit, as is letting go of the baggage of the past. This approach offers you the freedom to run your race with nothing weighing you down or holding you back.

Yesterday does not have to dictate tomorrow. You have the option to leave the hurts and sins of the past behind and fully grasp Jesus' hand as you move into your future. That's what Paul did.

If anyone had valid reasons to sink into the miry quicksand of guilt, it was Paul. After all, he had ruthlessly orchestrated the deaths of countless innocent Christians. In his religiosity and zeal, he had killed the Lord's own children.

How in the world could he live with himself? There was only one way – he had to relinquish all control and live the remainder of his life in harmony with the wishes of his Savior, Jesus Christ. He had to trust in Christ's ability to forgive his sins and wash him clean of unrighteousness. The same is true for you and me.

In the epiphany he experienced on the road to Damascus, Saul's estimate of himself was completely demolished. A self-righteous Jew of privileged background and impeccable credentials, he had been reduced to a monster. Can you imagine the shame and guilt that overcame him in that moment of realization?

In the same moment that Saul fully recognized the hopeless wretchedness of his life, he was given the greatest gift anyone could be given – a chance to know the living Christ personally and receive forgiveness for his sins. This gave him the courage to face himself for the sinner he was and reach out to a perfect Savior.

Saul had the strength to face his own evilness, because in that flash of insight he very personally felt the love of a holy and perfect Christ. Regardless of how disastrous his choices had been, he had a fresh chance to live in a way that brought purpose, satisfaction, and happiness to his life and to the lives of innumerable others. Saul received a new name, Paul, to commemorate the depth of meaning in this new beginning.

Paul was strong enough and humble enough to receive immediate and total forgiveness. This forgiveness is available to you right now if you will only believe in the risen Christ. Feel Christ's boundless love and receive it for yourself.

Realize there are no second-class citizens. You are not second-class no matter how vile your sins.

God chose Paul to take the Good News of Jesus Christ to the Gentiles. As a Jew, Saul had looked down at the Gentiles with great scorn. Now they would become the precious recipients of all he had discovered in Christ.

I imagine Paul's view of himself traversed through three lines of thought very quickly. He went from (1) an arrogant Pharisee, highly privileged in birth and ethical standing, to (2) a despicable murderer of God's people, to (3) a grateful sinner saved by the grace of Jesus Christ.

Though Paul was an undeserving sinner, God declared him "not guilty." In Romans 4: 7-8, Paul reflected on how centuries before, David had said, "Blessed and to be envied are those whose sins are forgiven and put out of sight. Yes, what joy there is for anyone whose sins are no longer counted against him by the Lord."

When we think of King David, a man after God's own heart, we can find hope for our own lives. I am sure Paul could relate to David's laundry list of sins, including the murder of Bathsheba's first husband.

David looked to a higher source for his security. After coming face to face with his own sinfulness, he sang, "O, God in Zion, we wait before you in silent praise, and thus fulfill our vow. And because you answer prayer, all mankind will come to you with their requests. Though sins fill our hearts, you forgive them all. How greatly to be envied are those you have chosen to come and live with you within the holy tabernacle courts! What joy awaits us among all the good things there." (Psalm 65: 1-4)

How could sinners such as David, Paul, you, and me find lasting happiness? Paul wrote in Romans 3: 2324, "Yes, all have sinned; all fall short of God's glorious ideal; yet God declares us not guilty of offending him if we trust in Jesus Christ, who in his kindness freely takes away your sins."

When God takes away our sins He does it absolutely and completely, removing them as far from us as the east is from the west. (see Psalm 103:12) He remembers them no more.

The realization of this glorious truth brings with it ultimate joy. It is a transforming moment when we discern that eternal salvation came through

Christ's suffering on the cruel cross. We need only to believe and it will be so, despite any sinful mess we may have made of our lives. This is the happiness Paul refers to in Philippians 4: 4-7:

"Always be full of joy in the Lord; I say it again, rejoice! Let everyone see that you are unselfish and considerate in all you do. Remember that the Lord is coming soon. Don't worry about anything, instead pray about everything; tell God your needs, and don't forget to thank him for his answers. If you do this, you will experience God's peace, which is far more wonderful than the human mind could understand. His peace will keep your thoughts and your hearts quiet and at rest as you trust in Christ Jesus."

Paul also wrote in Colossians 2: 4-7 about the joy found through new life with Christ: "For though I am far away from you my heart is with you, happy because you are getting along so well, happy because of your strong faith in Christ. And now, just as you trusted Christ to save you, trust him, too, for each day's problems; live in vital union with him. Let your roots grow down deep into him and draw up nourishment from him. See that you go on growing in the Lord, and become strong and vigorous in the truth you were taught. Let your lives overflow with joy and thanksgiving for all he has done."

Paul knew how to thrive. He grew to be content in whatever circumstances he found himself. Instead of complaining, he looked for a way to make the most of each situation. He viewed even the most treacherous of situations as opportunities.

We can learn how to conduct our own lives in the courageous and fulfilling manner Paul demonstrated. No matter what we have done and no matter what has been done to us, we, too, can have a joyful life with a happy ending. Don't miss all the bright and beautiful things in store for you when you are living in dynamic fusion with the Lord.

Paul was a perfect example of a strong and vigorous believer. His circumstances were often far from ideal, yet he always managed to be full of faith. He was beaten, brutalized, and imprisoned. It is said that some of his writings occurred when he was in a prison knee-high in sewage. Yet he kept the faith. He was happy because he had Jesus. He knew nothing and no one could ever take Jesus away.

Once while Paul and Silas were imprisoned, they were praying and singing hymns to the Lord around midnight when an earthquake occurred. The prison was shaken to its foundation. The cell doors flew open, and all of the prisoners' chains fell off. The guard awoke and assumed all the prisoners had escaped. So he drew his sword to kill himself. Paul yelled to the man not to kill himself. "We are all here," he assured the jailer.

The guard was so impressed and grateful that he fell before Paul and Silas and asked what he must do to be saved. They told him and his household the Good News – they could receive salvation by believing on the Lord Jesus. After washing the stripes on Paul and Silas's backs, the jailer and his family were baptized. They all shared a meal and rejoiced together.

Happiness is perhaps most sweet when we get to impact another human being's life for eternity. Paul and Silas found joy by giving the jailer and his family the greatest possible gift - a life lived in communion with Jesus Christ. How loving and thoughtful Paul and Silas were, even in the midst of their own suffering.

It was the attitude these brave heroes displayed that made them so effective. Paul described our bodies as perishable containers holding "this light and power that now shine within us" as precious treasure. This glorious power within is from God.

Paul buffeted his body. He disciplined his physical self just as he gloried in having Jesus in his heart. He said, "We are pressed on every side by troubles, but not crushed and broken. We are perplexed because we don't know why things happen as they do, but we don't give up and quit." (2 Corinthians 4:8)

Paul was wise enough to lubricate the irritations of his life with God's love. It is through such a process that a clam creates a pearl within itself. Think about the things in your life that irritate you. How can you surround (lubricate) these things in love?

Have you ever thought you could transform every day into a pearl of a day? How? Make conscious contact with God through prayer. Pray for guidance in the morning and pray with gratitude at night. Give each of your days to God for his purposes. In this way you can make your life into a strand of pearls – many days lived well unto the Lord.

Paul demonstrated this way of thinking when he said, "Not that I was ever in need, for I have learned how to get along happily whether I have much or little. I know how to live on almost nothing or with everything. I have learned the secret of contentment in every situation, whether it be a full stomach or hunger, plenty or want; for I can do everything God asks me to with the help of Christ who gives me the strength and power." (Philippians 4: 11-13)

A significant theme threads its way through the book of Philippians: Blessedness does not come from outward circumstances but rather from inward strength. Joy comes from knowing Christ personally and from depending on His power on a daily basis.

True happiness, Paul taught us, comes from turning our wants, needs, and indeed, our very lives, over to God in complete obedience. In Romans 12: 1-2 he exhorted, "I beseech you therefore, brethren by the mercies of God, that you present your bodies as a living sacrifice, holy, acceptable to God, which is your reasonable service. And do not be conformed to this world, but be transformed by the renewing of your mind, that you may prove what is that good and acceptable and perfect will of God." (NKJV)

Paul understood that we are good and acceptable only because we have Christ within. In Romans 7: 18 he wrote, "I know I am rotten through and through so far as my own sinful nature is concerned. No matter which way I turn, I can't make myself do right. I want to but I can't."

Paul demonstrated great humility in his writings. Paul, former torturer and murderer of Christians, was the supreme example showing that it is never too late while we are still here on Earth to exchange hubris for humility.

Thank God for the crucifixion of Jesus Christ and all that it meant! Romans 6:6 stated, "Your old evil desires were nailed to the cross with him; that part of you that loves to sin was crushed and fatally wounded, so that your sin-loving body is no longer under sin's control, no longer needs to be a slave to sin."

Galatians 5:24 concurred, "Those who belong to Christ have nailed their natural desires to his cross and crucified them there."

What was God accomplishing with creation? How was He saving His creation through the life and death of His only begotten son? Acts 17:27 explained, "His purpose in all of this is that they should seek after God and perhaps feel their way toward him and find him – though he is not far from any of us."

Seeking after God is a lifetime endeavor. It will involve, as it did for Paul, considerable suffering. However, if we depend on the Holy Spirit to testify from within, we, like Paul, can finish the race with joy. It can be for us as it was for Paul.

He put it this way: "Therefore we also, since we are surrounded by so great a cloud of witnesses, let us lay aside every weight, and the sin which so easily ensnares us, and let us run with endurance the race that is set before us, looking unto Jesus, the author and finisher of our faith, who for the joy that was set before Him endured the cross, despising the shame, and has sat down at the right hand of the throne of God." (Hebrews 12: 1-2 NKJV)

Paul's deep and penetrating devotion to Jesus made him happy. Why do you think this is so? Research has shown why, said Martin Seligman: "The data on the positive psychological effects of faith started to provide a countervailing force. Religious Americans are clearly less likely to abuse drugs, commit crimes, divorce, and kill themselves...The increase in optimism which increasing religiousness brings is entirely accounted for by greater hope...The relation of hope for the future and religious faith is probably the cornerstone of why faith so effectively fights despair and increases happiness."5

Living in this way elevates your mind, health, and general level of well-being. Break free from daily stressors and focus on the little things in life that bring you joy. An aptitude for happiness is as available for you as it was for Paul.

You can take small steps to a healthier and happier life. One of the best habits you can cultivate is the ability to focus on your strengths and pay scant attention to your weaknesses. There are also other easy ways to promote health and happiness.

Simplifying your life, for instance, can increase happiness. Feeling like you have enough time to pursue the things you want to pursue is a better indicator of a satisfied life than income. The term for this is *time affluence.*

Do you take time to draw away from your work and refresh yourself? Jesus withdrew often to pray and receive power form His Father.

You might be interested to know that while it is positive to achieve a reasonable quality of life, beyond a basic level of financial security, money does not bring happiness. Possessions will not bring lasting fulfillment.

Taking time to develop a hobby can make you happier. It increases your satisfaction and self-esteem. When you are creative, you become more flexible and open.

Have you ever become totally absorbed and focused while working on a hobby or participating in a sport? Positive psychologist Dr. Csikszentmihalyi refers to this heightened state of consciousness as *flow.* Finding activities you love that put you in a state of flow is relaxing and enjoyable.

If you want to be happy, it is helpful to not continually seek out the very best decision in every area of your life. Make the best choice you can and then move on. Continually revisiting decisions creates anxiety. Good enough is good enough. Becoming a perfectionist is counterproductive. We must do the best we can at the time and be satisfied with that.

Consider widening your circle of friends. All kinds of positive relationships with others can contribute significantly to the level of happiness you experience. It is great to have some acquaintances to chat with for a few minutes. It is also quite fulfilling to have bosom buddies with whom to share innermost secrets.

Forgetting your own problems to help someone else is among the most effective strategies to becoming happy. Doing a good deed resonates within your heart much longer than if you had spent the time in a more frivolous manner. Practice altruism and watch your life satisfaction take a leap in the positive direction.

Bring happiness into your life through realizing that some people will not like you. Don't take everyone's judgment to heart. I once heard it said that ten percent of people will not like you no matter what. Don't surrender your own ability to view yourself clearly or at least compassionately.

Think more about your accomplishments than your defeats. Remind yourself of times when people you respect complimented you. It is amazing how much we needlessly torture ourselves about past mistakes rather than moving on to greater levels of happiness.

You can distract yourself from negative self-talk through exercise. This will strengthen your mind and body. Exercise increases fitness, enhances the way chemicals flow through your brain, and develops greater life satisfaction.

Happiness combines self-satisfaction, general contentment, and the ability to enjoy life. Strive for cheerfulness and enthusiasm. It is important to have dreams and be willing to take risks, if only on a modest scale. Choose to derive pleasure and meaning from what you do. Stay in balance to keep feeling good.

Reflect on how happy and resilient Paul became after his encounter with Christ on the road to Damascus. He wanted to share the Good News with as many people as possible. We can see a similar change of heart toward others in Zacchaeus' life.

In the beginning, Zacchaeus, the tax collector, was very unhappy. He absconded with as much of other peoples' money as he could. But that lifestyle did not work well for him. It had not brought him joy. So he climbed the highest tree he could find in hope of glimpsing Jesus as He passed.

Various aspects of our lives can converge to make us, like Zacchaeus, unhappy people. Sometimes we have unrealistic expectations. Perhaps we want to get something we desire without putting in the necessary effort. We cannot bypass the hard work of obtaining the knowledge and skill needed to achieve our goal legitimately.

Other times we feel so deflated that we completely give up on our goals and dreams. This can cause us to feel helpless and hopeless. We can correct this situation by modifying our expectations, setting reasonable goals and having a little bit of faith in ourselves.

A useful tool that will help you move toward victory is an understanding and application of emotional intelligence. It is important to understand what motivates you and what motivates others. Emotional intelligence arises through being observant of people and listening carefully to what they say. It also means being in touch with what you are thinking and feeling in the moment.

My friend Elizabeth has emotional intelligence. She makes friends wherever she goes. She was on a bus once and heard a blind lady talking about how much it was going to cost to pay someone to paint the interior of her home. Elizabeth offered to do it for free on the spot. She followed through, and cleaned weekly for that woman and another blind couple for several years.

Elizabeth has done missionary work with Native American children and in Haiti, South Africa, and India. When she goes on these trips she takes all the luggage she can, filled with things like clothes and shoes to leave for the people she encounters. She comes home pleased and empty handed.

She is a bike enthusiast. She can log a great many miles at a time. The energy she generates through healthy exercise is infectious and she strives to help anyone in need who happens to cross her path.

She is other-centered. After his encounter with Jesus, Zacchaeus became other-centered too. He became an example of transformation from a person of greed to person who wanted to give back:

"Then Jesus entered and passed through Jericho. Now behold, there was a man named Zacchaeus who was a chief tax collector, and he was rich. And he sought to see who Jesus was, but could not because of the crowd, for he was short in stature. So he ran ahead and climbed up into a sycamore tree to see Him, for He was going to pass that way. And when Jesus came to the place, He looked up and saw him and said to him, 'Zacchaeus, make haste and come down, for today I must stay at your house.' So he made haste and came down, and received Him joyfully. But when they saw it, they all complained, saying, 'He has gone to be a guest with a man who is a sinner.' Then Zacchaeus stood and said to the Lord, 'Look, Lord, I give half of my goods to the poor, and if I have taken anything from anyone by false accusation, I restore fourfold.' And Jesus said to him, 'Today salvation has come to this house, because he is a son of Abraham; for the Son of Man has come to seek and to save that which was lost.'" (Luke 19: 1-10 NKJV)

Zacchaeus had earned a reputation as a swindler. But in the twinkling of an eye, he went from being unscrupulous and greedy to loving and giving. The Living Word cries out through Zacchaeus' life, as it does through Paul's, pointing out that no one is so despicable that he or she cannot be completely transformed through Jesus Christ's love and mercy. Along with Zacchaeus and Saul (Paul), join the ranks of errant human beings acutely aware of just how much we need a perfect Savior:

"The Lord [earnestly] waits [expecting, looking, and longing] to be gracious to you; and therefore He lifts Himself up, that He may have mercy on you and show loving-kindness to you. For the Lord is a God of justice. Blessed (happy, fortunate, to be envied) are all those who [earnestly] wait for Him, who expect and look and long for Him [for His victory, His favor, His love, His peace, His joy, and His matchless, unbroken companionship]." (Isaiah 30:18 AMP)

How can we ever know the end of happiness once we grasp the reality of Jesus' unbroken companionship? If we are Christians, we will joyfully fellowship together forever and ever.

8 THE EVERLASTING STORY

"Promise Yourself

"To be so strong that nothing can disturb your peace of mind. To talk health, happiness, and prosperity to every person you meet.

"To make all your friends feel that there is something in them. To look at the sunny side of everything and make your optimism come true.

"To think only the best, to work only for the best, and to expect only the best. To be just as enthusiastic about the success of others as you are about your own.

"To forget the mistakes of the past and press on to the greater achievements of the future. To wear a cheerful countenance at all times and give every living creature you meet a smile.

"To give so much time to the improvement of yourself that you have no time to criticize others. To be too large for worry, too noble for anger, too strong for fear, and too happy to permit the presence of trouble.

"To think well of yourself and to proclaim this fact to the world, not in loud words but great deeds. To live in faith that the whole world is on your side so long as you are true to the best that is in you."

— Christian D. Larson, *Your Forces and How to Use Them*

This world deserves the best that is within you. You deserve to achieve the best that is within you. God is giving you this chance – a short time on planet Earth – to give it all you've got to achieve the best that is within you.

Eternal rewards await those who leave all impediments behind and passionately go all out for the Gospel of Jesus Christ. This book has shown examples of people in the Bible who gave their very best – Job, Solomon, Mary (Jesus's mother), Simon Peter, Mary Magdalene, a leper, Paul, and Zacchaeus.

In God's everlasting story, perhaps someday in heaven we'll have the honor of sitting down with these people. Their stories and our stories will funnel into the flux of the Great Story that will go on forever.

Chapter two probed the story of Job and the sublime patience he exhibited while going through extreme pain and suffering that he did not understand. Job was a good and faithful man, yet he dealt with excruciating afflictions that had no apparent reasons or explanations.

Through his various calamities – losing his family and his wealth, being struck with horrific boils, being accused of great sins from his so-called friends, and basically being told by his wife to "curse God and die" – Job never quit believing in God and His goodness.

Somehow Job made it through his terrible ordeal, communicating to God throughout it all. He steadfastly refused to give up on his Creator. In the end, God restored everything that Job had lost. Job ended up with much more than he had forfeited.

Job's story can give us solace when we are suffering deeply and do not understand why. Like Job, we must acknowledge that God is much higher than us. His ways are sometimes beyond our finite comprehension.

We must be mindful of the fact that God has His reasons and that He is good – all the time. Like Job, we can cry out to Him, express our pain, and ultimately trust Him saying, "Though He slay me, yet I will trust Him."

Henri J.M. Nouwen said, "A waiting person is a patient person. The word patience means the willingness to stay where we are and live the situation out to the full in the belief that something hidden there will manifest itself to us."

Fulton J. Sheen once stated, "Patience is power. Patience is not an absence of action; rather it is 'timing,' it waits on the right time to act, for the right principles and in the right way."

Aristotle summed it up beautifully, "Patience is bitter, but its fruit is sweet."

Chapter three penetrated the saga of Solomon and his great desire for wisdom as a leader and a true believer. Solomon was smart even before he received God's help because he was astute enough to request God's wisdom when God offered him anything he wished. Solomon did not ask for fame or fortune. He desired above all to rule Israel proficiently and judiciously.

God granted Solomon's wish and gave him the gift of great wisdom. This truth hit home to me when I looked up the word "wise" in *Sisson's Synonyms* and found the terms "Solomnian" and "Solomonic" listed.

King Solomon wrote the Proverbs to share his great acumen with the people he governed. His words are still relevant and spot-on to readers today. Many great Biblical teachers encourage believers to read a chapter in Proverbs each day. Since there are 31 chapters, a person could read through Proverbs completely in a month in this manner.

There is so much common sense in the book of Proverbs. But part of the reason we can refer to its wisdom as "common" is because it is available for us in the Old Testament.

As we look forward to the day when we will dwell everlastingly with our Father, we can find solace in the words of Alexandre Dumas as he speaks about wisdom: "There is neither happiness nor misery in the world: There is only the comparison of one state with another, nothing more. He who has felt the deepest grief is best able to experience supreme happiness. We must have felt what it is to die, that we may appreciate the enjoyments of life. Live, then, and be happy, beloved children of my heart, and never forget, that until the day God will deign to reveal the future to man, all human wisdom is contained in these two words, 'Wait and Hope.'"

Chapter four juxtaposed the peace Jesus's mother, Mary, exhibited with the evil paranoia of King Herod. Mary was a very young girl when Gabriel appeared to her to tell her she had been chosen to be the mother of the Messiah.

Almost immediately, Mary embraced all Gabriel revealed with a pure heart that desired the fulfillment of God's will above anything else. Throughout her motherhood experience, Mary portrayed a dignity filled with quiet grace. Coping with being a pregnant virgin was preparation for the toughest experience of her life – the day she had to watch her perfect Son be crucified on a rugged cross.

There are almost no adequate words to describe the grief and pain she experienced that day. She had the great honor of being chosen among all women to be the Savior's mother. But, oh, how high the price she had to pay. She had to watch as He was mocked, scorned, and abused. She was forced to stand helplessly by and watch the brutality of his crucifixion. Mary never failed to demonstrate composure in the most difficult of circumstances.

Saint Frances de Sales said, "Never be in a hurry; do everything quietly and in a calm spirit. Do not lose your inner peace for anything whatsoever, even if your whole world seems upset."

Fred Rogers, a minister who exhibited great calm and serenity for years on his children's show, commented, "When I say it's you I like, I'm talking about that part of you that knows that life is far more than anything you can ever see or hear or touch. That deep part of you that allows you to stand for things without which humankind cannot survive. Love that conquers hate, peace that rises triumphant over war, and justice that proves more powerful than greed."

Chapter five explored the enthusiasm and commitment of Simon Peter. It is impossible to think of Peter and not think of passion.

Harriet Tubman once said, "Every great dream begins with a dreamer. Always remember you have within you the strength, the patience, and the passion to reach for the stars to change the world."

Peter lived large. He attempted to walk on the water to Jesus. He adamantly disputed that he would ever deny Jesus, then loudly did it three times. He recovered to bring in the presence of the Holy Spirit at Pentecost.

The strengths of enthusiasm and commitment are vital in setting and achieving goals. Thinking about our goals is vital. If we don't have concrete goals, we will flounder and stumble. If we write out our specific aims and review them often, we have a good chance of achieving them. Visualizing these goals and even writing them out several times daily can assist us in believing that we can obtain that which we desire.

Of goals, Louisa May Alcott commented, "Far away there in the sunshine are my highest aspirations. I may not reach them, but I can look up and see their beauty, believe in them, and try to follow where they lead."

Though Peter made many mistakes, he achieved some amazing feats. An uneducated fisherman, he became a zealous preacher who boldly and eloquently shared the Good News of Jesus Christ.

Like Peter, we should declare the truth of the Gospel with all the enthusiasm and commitment we can muster. Like Peter, we must shine brightly in professing the healing redemption available in trusting our Lord, Jesus.

Chapter six discussed the marvelous trait of gratitude. Mary Magdalene beautifully exhibited gratitude when she washed Jesus' feet with expensive perfume and wiped them with her hair. Jesus explained that those who understand they can be totally forgiven for all their numerous and heinous sins are extremely thankful. Such grace is an almost unbelievable truth. Because of what Jesus did for us on the cross, we can be released from our otherwise damning transgressions.

Another great story of gratitude toward Jesus is that of the healed Samaritan leper found in Luke 17. Jesus had healed ten lepers, yet only one returned to thank Him. Interestingly, it was the solitary non-Jew among them. He was a Samaritan – an alien in Israel – but singularly returned to express his great appreciation to Christ.

Gratitude can go a long way in helping us heal from our emotional wounds.

When we fully fathom the vastness of God's love for us, how else could we possibly respond but with joyfulness?

Chapter four of Revelation gives us an exquisite vision of the gratitude continually expressed in heaven: "Each of these living beings had six wings, and their wings were covered all over with eyes, inside and out. Day after day and night after night they kept on saying, 'Holy, holy, holy is the Lord God, the Almighty – the One who always was, who is, and who is still to come.' Whenever the living beings give glory and honor and thanks to the one sitting on the throne (the one who lives forever and ever), the twenty-four elders fall down and worship the one sitting on the throne (The one who lives forever and ever). And they lay their crowns before the throne and say, 'You are worthy, O Lord our God, to receive glory and honor and power. For You created all things, and they exist because You created what You pleased.'" (Revelation 4: 8-11)

Chapter seven celebrated happiness. Dale Carnegie wrote in *How to Win Friends and Influence People*, "It isn't what you have or who you are or where you are or what you are doing that makes you happy or unhappy. It is what you think about it."

If we put our minds on the gloriousness of God and the possibility of communion with Him, joy will overflow from within our souls. Bitterness and emotional scars can be overcome when we trust in Jesus. He alone can raise us out of our troubles and set us firmly on the road to happiness.

It is definitely worthwhile to infuse more positive emotions into our everyday lives. Evoking positivity makes us healthier and hardier in a myriad of ways. Paul is a great study of happiness found in the New Testament. From a Damascus road conversion experience, he was transformed from a Pharisee who brutally hunted down Christians to a sold-out believer in Jesus who would pay any price to tell the world about the salvation that could be found only in Jesus Christ.

Let's examine what Paul wrote in Philippians 4: 10-13 in two different translations to get the full flavor of the passage's meaning. The *Message* version states: "I'm glad in God, far happier than you would ever guess – happy that you're again showing such strong concern for me. Not that you ever quit praying and thinking about me. You just had no chance to show it. Actually, I don't have a sense of needing anything personally. I've learned by now to be quite content whatever my circumstance. I'm just as happy with little as with much, with much as with little. I've found the recipe for being happy whether full or hungry, hands full or hands empty. Whatever I have, wherever I am, I can make it through anything in the One who makes me who I am."

The *Amplified* version put it this way: "I was made very happy in the Lord that now you have revived your interest in my welfare after so long a time; you were indeed thinking of me, but you had no opportunity to show it. Not that I am implying that I was in any personal want, for I have learned how to be content (satisfied to the point where I am not disturbed or disquieted) in whatever state I am. I know how to be abased and live humbly in straitened circumstances, and I know also how to enjoy plenty and live in abundance. I have learned in any and all circumstances the secret of facing every situation, whether well-fed or going hungry, having a sufficiency and enough to spare or going without and being in want. I have strength for all things in Christ who empowers me [I am ready for anything and equal to anything through Him who infuses inner strength into me; I am self-sufficient in Christ's sufficiency]."

Like Paul, one of our deepest desires is to be self-sufficient in Christ's sufficiency. This is what makes for a happy life.

Zacchaeus' story, too, teaches us about true felicity. After a divine encounter with the living Christ, he morphed from a deceitful, greedy man to a magnanimous, generous, joyous and free person. This is the power of having Jesus in our hearts and lives. This is redemption. This is blessed solace.

The stories we have examined in this book can help us more deeply comprehend how very much we need our omnipotent God. Like Job, we can grow to understand that, even though we don't understand intense suffering, God does understand and will someday restore us to wholeness. Like Solomon, we must never cease to seek God's unfathomable wisdom. Like Jesus' mother, Mary, we must acquiesce to God's will, no matter what the cost or how much it hurts. Like Simon Peter, we ought to be zealous about telling others the Good News about Jesus Christ and what He has done for us. Like Mary Magdalene and the cleansed leper, our hearts should overflow with gratitude to our dear, loving Savior. Like Paul and Zacchaeus, we should be so happy in Jesus that our joy spills out and overflows to others.

In the eternal stream of time, the stories of these captivating Bible characters and our own individual stories will merge and intertwine. We are all a part of God's great epic – a majestic, everlasting story.

ENDNOTES

Chapter 2

1Mark Brazee, 31 Days of Healing (Tulsa: Harrison House, 2003), 25.

2Ibid.

3Ibid., 26-27.

4Stephen Arterburn and David Stoop, eds., The Life Recovery Bible (Wheaton, Illinois: Tyndale, 1992), 591.

5Billy Graham, The Holy Spirit: Activating God's Power in Your Life (Nashville: Word Publishing), 259.

6Arterburn, 564.

7Wikipedia on the World Wide Web, (2008).

8Ibid.

9Ibid.

10Ibid.

11Jim Rohn, Patience, Jim Rohn's Weekly E-zine (accessed June 30, 2008).

12Mihaly Csikszentmihalyi and Jeanne Nakamura, "The Concept of Flow," in Handbook of Positive Psychology, eds., C.R. Snyder and Shane Lopez, 89-105 (USA: Oxford University Press, 2002) 95.

13Ibid.

14Ibid.

15Dan Baker and Cathy Greenburg, What Happy Women Know (USA: Rodale, 2007),xiii.

16Robert Emmons, "Personal Goals, Life Meaning, and Virtue: Wellsprings of a Positive Life," in Flourishing: Positive Psychology and the Life Well-Lived, eds., Corey Keyes and Jonathan Haidt, 105-128 (Washington D.C.: APA, 2003) 121.

17Ibid., 121-22.

18Charles Carver and Michael Scheier, "Three Human Strengths, "in A Psychology of Human Strengths: Fundamental Questions and Future

Directions for a Positive Psychology, eds., Lisa Aspinwall and Ursula Staudinger, 87-102 (Washington D.C.: APA, 2003) 88.

19Ibid., 89.

20Rick Renner, Sparkling Gems from the Greek (Tulsa: Teach All Nations, 2003) 641.

Chapter 3

1Jenifer Westphal quoted in Dan Baker and Cathy Greenburg, What Happy Wormen Know (USA: Rodale, 2007) 225.

2Ute Kunzmann, "Approaches to a Good Life: The Emotional-Motivational Side to Wisdom," in Positive Psychology in Practice, eds. P. Alex Lindley and Stephen Joseph, 504-517 (USA, Wiley, 2004) 504.

3Ibid., 511.

4Wikepedia on the World Wide Web, (2008).

5Steven Scott, The Richest Man Who Ever Lived: King Solomon's Secrets to Success, Wealth, and Happiness (USA, Waterbrook Press, 2006) 2.

6Paul Baltes, Judith Gluck, and Ute Kunzmann, "Wisdom: Its Structure and Functionin Regualting Successful Life Span Development," in Handbook of Positive Psychology, eds. C.R. Snyder and Shane Lopez, 327-347 (New York: Oxford Univeristy Press, 2002) 331.

7Ibid., 330, Table 24.

8Scott, 12.

9Ibid., 53.

10Ibid., 251.

11Wikepedia on the World Wide Web, (2008).

12Ibid., 264.

13John Maxwell, "Lessons from Basketball's Greatest Coach," Eric Musselman's Basketball Notebook, emuss.blogspot.com (accessed July 29, 2008).

Chapter 4

1Dan Baker and Cathy Greenberg, What Happy Women Know: How

New Findings in Positive Psychology can Change Women's Lives for the Better (New York: Rodale, 2007), 13.

2Nancy Eisenberg and Vivian Ota Wang, "Toward a Positive Psychology: Social Developmental and Cultural Contributions," in A Psychology of Human Strengths; Fundamental Questions and Future Directions for a Positive Psychology, eds. Lisa Aspinwall and Ursula Staudnigner, 117-129 (Washington D.C., APA, 2003), 123.

3L.Quisumbing, "A Framework for Teacher Education programmes in Asia and the Pacific," in Korean Nation Commission for UNESCO's Education for International Understanding and Peace in Asia and the Pacific,108-120 (Bangkok, Thailand: UNESCO Principal Regional Office for Asia and the Pacific, 1999), 110-111.

Chapter 5

1Edwin Locke, "Setting Goals for Life and Happiness," in Handbook of Positive Psychology, eds. C.R. Snyder and Shane Lopez, 299-312 (New York: Oxford, 2002), 305.

2Christopher Peterson and Nansook Park, "Classification and Measurement of Character Strengths: Implications for Practice," in Positive Psychology in Practice eds. P. Alex Linley and Stephen Joseph, 433-446 (USA: Wiley, 2004), 437.

3Martin Seligman, Authentic Happiness: Using the New Positive Psychology to Realize Your Potential for Lasting Fulfillment (New York: Free Press. 2002), 13.

Chapter 6

1Emmit Miller in M.J. Ryan, Attitudes of Gratitude: How to Give and Receive Joy Every Day of Your Life (New York: MFJ Books, 1999),73.

2Giacomo Bono, Robert Emmons, and Michael McCullough, "Gratitude in Practice and the Practice of Gratitude," in Positive Psychology in Practice, eds. P. Alex Linley and Stephen Joseph, 464-481 (USA: Wiley, 2004), 464.

3Ryan, 5.

4Chris Widener, "Attitudes of Successful Learners," Chris Widener's Ezine, Issue no. 83. Accessed March 26, 2008.

5Bono, 477.

Chapter 7

[1]Martin Seligman, *Authentic Happiness: Using the New Positive Psychology to Realize Your Potential for Lasting Fulfillment* (New York: Free Press, 2002), 13.

[2]Ibid., 43.

[3]Ibid., 35.

[4]Ibid., 41.

[5]Ibid., 59.

ABOUT THE AUTHOR

Kimberly Mittendorf Hensley is a writer and certified life coach. She is a licensed professional counselor with a BFA in theatre and Master's degrees in community counseling and the education of people with disabilities.

She is a certified Coach and Master Coach in Self Confidence by The Center for Personal Reinvention. She is also a certified Life Coach from the American Union of Neuro-Linguistic Programming.

She has received certificates in Life Coaching through Light University and the American Association of Christian Counselors (AACC) equaling 87 hours of training. She has also completed 27 modules from the AACC on *The Blessing Project: Creating a Culture of Blessing in Your Home and with Others*.

Kimberly has also completed continuing education in several Shakespeare classes, Disability studies, The Art of Public Speaking, The Art of Teaching, Positive Psychology, and the Old and New Testaments. She is a graduate of the Jerry B. Jenkins Christian Writer's Guild Journeyman Program.

While working at Clermont Counseling Center from 1997- 2005, she gave over forty speeches at various conferences and meetings. She created and implemented a consumer medication education curriculum. She also created and implemented a positive psychology program entitled, *Claim Your Strengths; Reclaim Your Life*.

Kimberly's book, *Applying Inspiring Biographies from the Bible for Personal Growth*, was published in 2015, This book, *Applying More Inspiring Biographies from the Bible for Personal Growth*, is a companion to that book. Yet to come are *Friendship: The Heartbeat of Love* and *Our Wonderful Three-in-One God*.

Kimberly is currently writing *Enjoying Reading: Think, Learn, and Grow for a Lifetime*. She is also working on a book entitled, *Everybody Has Needs: A Positive Christian Approach for People with Disabilities and Their Caregivers*.

Kimberly foresees creating and performing a play portraying *The*

Women of Jesus.

Kimberly was selected as the Outstanding Graduate of the University of Cincinnati Community Counseling Program of 2002. She received the Wasserman Champion Award from the Clermont County Mental Health and Recovery Board in 2003.

Dear reader,
You would help me greatly by reviewing this book on Amazon.com. Thank you for your support.

I would love to hear from you. My email address is khensley@zoomtown.com. My website is www.supportbykim.com. I am a certified life coach. Please let me know how I can help you.

My next book, *Friendship: The Heartbeat of Love*, will be available soon. I hope you will look for it.

Blessings,
Kimberly

Made in the USA
Charleston, SC
28 December 2016